Twin sisters Lily and Rose Carter are done with men! Rose's divorce and Lily's breakup have seen to that. Their careers at Evergreen General Hospital and their shared house, a cat and each other are all they need, right?

Except they are in for a twin surprise!

In *A Daddy for Her Babies*

Dr. Lily Carter is good friends with colleague Dr. Theo Montgomery. And while a chemistry zings between them, she's not prepared to do anything about it. She doesn't need another guy who's big on dating but not on commitment. Except when she discovers she's pregnant with twins, he's the rock she never expected...

In *From a Fling to a Family*

Fertility doctor Rose Carter might not want a man, but she does want a family. And she's determined to become a mom via IVF. But meeting new ob-gyn Dr. Lucas Bennett changes all that. Now she's pregnant with twins—are her babies a result of the IVF or is their father kind, caring Lucas, who challenges all her views?

Both titles available now.

Dear Reader,

I always dreamed of having a twin sister who knew me inside out and whose clothes I could steal. When it came to writing the first book in this Twin Baby Bumps duet, starring one of our "flower girl" twins, pediatric nurse Lily Carter, I was even more excited to throw a hot doctor into the mix. Add in the drama of a surprise pregnancy and a friends-to-lovers entanglement, and this might be one of my favorites yet! I hope you enjoy the journey through Chicago into...forever?

Becky Wicks

A DADDY FOR HER BABIES

BECKY WICKS

MEDICAL ROMANCE

Harlequin®
MEDICAL ROMANCE

Recycling programs for this product may not exist in your area.

ISBN-13: 978-1-335-94306-4

A Daddy for Her Babies

Harlequin Enterprises ULC
22 Adelaide St. West, 41st Floor
Toronto, Ontario M5H 4E3, Canada
www.Harlequin.com

Printed in U.S.A.

Born in the UK, **Becky Wicks** has suffered interminable wanderlust from an early age. She's lived and worked all over the world, from London to Dubai, Sydney, Bali, New York City and Amsterdam. She's written for the likes of *GQ*, *Hello!*, *Fabulous* and *Time Out*, and has written a host of YA romance, plus three travel memoirs—*Burqalicious*, *Balilicious* and *Latinalicious* (HarperCollins, Australia). Now she blends travel with romance for Harlequin and loves every minute! Find her on Substack: @beckywicks.

Books by Becky Wicks

Harlequin Medical Romance

Falling Again for the Animal Whisperer
Fling with the Children's Heart Doctor
White Christmas with Her Millionaire Doc
A Princess in Naples
The Vet's Escape to Paradise
Highland Fling with Her Best Friend
South African Escape to Heal Her
Finding Forever with the Single Dad
Melting the Surgeon's Heart
A Marriage Healed in Hawaii
Tempted by the Outback Vet

Buenos Aires Docs

Daring to Fall for the Single Dad

Valentine Flings

Nurse's Keralan Temptation

Visit the Author Profile page
at Harlequin.com for more titles.

CHAPTER ONE

Outside, the Chicago rain is hammering at the windows like it's trying to match my heartbeat. The tiny infant is swaddled in a bundle of sheets, and his chest is heaving in erratic jerks in front of me. I feel the pull on my nerves at the thought that his next breath could be this baby's last, but today, with everything I've just learned, I'm walking a fine line, not letting the shock show on my face.

"O2 sats are dropping. We need to intubate!" I call out. As the specialist NICU pediatrician, I've been called down to the ER from neonatal. No one knows what I've just discovered upstairs in my own department's bathrooms. And no one will. "Theo?"

"On it, Doctor Carter." Theo's dashed through the doors with his coat still open as if he's only just started his shift. Dr. Theo Montgomery, the ER's chief resident, takes one look at the baby's skin and agrees we need to prep for intubation. The child is a canvas of mottled blues and grays, the colors no child should be. We work side by side on the baby, swiftly, calmly, even as my head spins. He looks at me questioningly when I drop a tube to the floor, and I know that look, because I know him. He's questioning why someone who knows this department as well as her own is so clumsy today.

You'd never know from seeing Theo like this that he boxes almost at a pro level, rides his bike over fifty miles most weekends, owns a penthouse apartment with barely anything in it, adores his niece, hates all cats—even mine—and knows all the words to ABBA's "Dancing Queen." But *I* know these things. I've learned them as a result of the past four years, working with him here at Evergreen General Hospital, self-medicating on coffee alongside him in the unflatteringly floodlit cafeteria and letting him tell me about his dates as Chicago's busiest bachelor. He's my friend, my ally.

Friends don't keep secrets like mine.

"Prepping for intubation," I say while he's orchestrating his own team like he always does, with the confidence of a maestro at the front of a concert hall.

"I'm on airway," I tell him. I glance up to meet his blue eyes, and I don't miss the way Amber, my assistant neonatologist who's come to help me, fans her coat at the collar, watching him. He's the epitome of collected determination in turquoise-green scrubs. His coat is ironed to crease-free perfection. Even under the unforgiving fluorescent lights, he's a sight to behold and he knows it. Outside Evergreen, his eyes can't seem to stay on one woman past the first date, and he never talks much about his family besides his niece, unlike me. I talk about Rose all the time. How could I not? She's my twin and we live together, but somehow over the years, Theo and I have connected on a platonic, colleagues-to-friends level that I appreciate. Which is why I have to tell him my secret. But I can't. I have to talk to Rose first, and the baby's father. Oh, Lord.

My hands position the laryngoscope. I guide the tube gently past the baby's vocal cords, and the rush of adrenaline is followed by a strange flush of heat that almost knocks me off my feet. My heart hasn't settled enough yet for this.

Concentrate, Lily.

"Tube's in place," I announce, securing it before looking up for Theo's nod of approval. He gives orders for medication and Amber scurries to follow my own commands. He and I, we're the calm in the storm, always have been at work. Outside, well, things can get crazy. I guess I started at Evergreen around the beginning of my "I'm single and I don't give a crap" phase, when I was doing anything and everything to get Grayson out of my system. Theo kind of took me under his wing. Well, I'm pretty sure he had his mind on hooking up with me, but I squished that plan pretty fast. He's the biggest flirt on earth, the last person I'd trust with my heart after Grayson, but we do have fun. And the reason I'm in this mess now is because I was having fun. These are the consequences of my actions. It was supposed to be a *fun* holiday, a *fun*, one-time, one-night-only hookup with a *fun* guy on a motorcycle...

"Where are we at, Doctor Carter?"

I tell him we're not out of the woods yet.

I do my best every day to make sure no woman's world has to fall apart, so that no one has to endure the crippling loss of a child. Theo saves adult lives every day. But Dr. Theo Montgomery has no idea how much my own foundations have just been rocked. What would he do if he saw the check marks on the three little sticks in my purse in my locker? Our so-called *fun* is about to stop for good. He won't want to hang out with a pregnant lady and I can't give it up, even though it was an accident. I can't; I'm thirty-four. What if I never get this chance again?

Looking back, I was ready to start trying for a baby five or six months after meeting Grayson, back when I truly felt he was the love of my life.

He certainly gave off those vibes at the start; no one knew the monster that lurked beneath the surface, especially not me! All I ever wanted was to love and care for and guide a child of my own, and that was what Grayson brought to the table, all packaged up in a wealthy, talented, handsome lover. I've often thought maybe I was blinded by my desire for a family when Grayson came along. If I'd looked harder, maybe I wouldn't have missed the sinister reality of what was really under my nose.

I draw up the precise dose of epinephrine, willing my hands not to shake as I pass the syringe to Theo. The infant's chest is tiny, so, so fragile, but he's fighting with each shallow breath. How big is the baby inside *me* at this point? No bigger than the nail on my little finger, already developing the tiny buds that'll be his or her arms and legs. He or she has a heartbeat. I'm growing another *life* inside me.

"Pushing one of epi," Theo announces, hands steady while the baby's heart dances wildly on the monitor.

"Come on, little guy," I whisper under my breath, taking his tiny hand between my fingers. The chaos begins to ebb, but the storm is far from over. I rub my eyes and blink a little too hard and catch Theo observing me. Concern etches lines in his forehead and I look away. He knows me; he already knows something's not right. His laser senses pick up on everything. At least he didn't see me almost walk into a glass door on the way in. My head was in the clouds. It still is, but now isn't the time to unravel.

"Blood gas next," I instruct, and he has it ready before I even finish my sentence. I take a swift sample from the baby's right heel. Theo nods, that familiar crease between his brows deepening.

"Oxygen saturation coming up," I report, watching the numbers climb slowly on the screen. "Heart rate's improving. Let's wean down the O2, see if he can hold his own."

Theo's gaze is fixed on the baby and I know he is willing him to fight, to stay with us. My hand goes briefly to my belly, just above my waistline, as I decrease the oxygen. The child's labored efforts soon ease into something resembling normalcy, but I'm still fighting to keep my emotions in check, seeing all this play out, knowing what's happening inside me in secret. "He's stabilizing."

There's a unanimous sigh of relief in the room. I can't stop the corner of my mouth from lifting, even as I swipe at my tired eyes. My head is starting to pound under these lights. Theo's blue eyes lock with mine for a heavy beat as he confirms we should get the baby up to NICU, the corners crinkling ever so slightly. He knows something's up. He definitely knows. So I really need to tell him.

It's at least an hour before he finds me, staring at my phone.

"Coffee, Carter?" he asks me from where he's snuck up, stealth-like, in the staff room. I ram my phone into my pocket too quickly, hiding the text I was writing to *Miami Motorhead*. I've written about nine drafts so far, but haven't sent anything yet. How do you tell a relative stranger several states away in Florida that he's impregnated you by mistake?

Theo turns those intense all-seeing eyes on me. "You okay? You're acting off today."

"Charming as usual," I say, feigning indifference to the way he's trying to read me. I search for a crease in the white lab coat over his scrubs. He's always so tidy. So meticulous. I tease him outside work. He has four pens in the breast pocket of his coat today, all lined up like soldiers ready for battle.

He steps closer and my breath hitches under his scrutiny. "I saw you zoning out." A faint trace of his cologne mingles with the antiseptic surroundings in my nostrils, and for a second I have to hold my breath. I usually like his woody sandalwood scent whenever I'm breathing it in, but it's making me feel a little ill right now.

"I'm just overtired," I tell him.

"Up late, drooling over warrior Highlanders again, were you?"

"If only I *could* time travel back to eighteenth-century Scotland. I wouldn't have to deal with you," I tell him quickly, and he smirks and cocks an eyebrow. Curse Rose for letting on in the cafeteria that we've been watching two old episodes of *Outlander* every night this week.

"Really, I'm fine, Theo." I sigh, trying to sound convincing. The July rain is still pounding the window in the periphery of my vision. He searches my face for a moment longer. Does he see through my facade? I should just tell him what I know right now…but I can't.

"Let's get you one of your frothy oat milk things," he says eventually. "You look like you could use it."

"Lead the way," I say, following him out of the room. What I really need is a moment alone to finish that text message, to wrap my head around the life growing inside me—a life that literally no one knows about except me. Rose is going to freak out, but I can't very well keep this from my twin. I can't keep anything from Rose, and not even just because we live together. I've a feeling she would know something was up with me if she lived on the moon, and I was still here on the outskirts of Chicago and we never spoke. Twin Spidey senses, and all that.

I never told her the first time Grayson started showcasing frightening narcissistic tendencies toward me, about a year into our relationship. I mean, there were red flags before that, but I pretended it wasn't happening at first, told myself I was imagining it, being paranoid. For the first eight to nine months I was completely head over heels. He was fun and complimentary, whisked me away on mini breaks, cooked me dinners, or tried to—he was never that good, even though I told him he was. He made everything too salty. That was the trigger, actually. When I told him his carbonara was too salty. It sounds so silly to say now, but the look on his face when I said that—that was the moment he changed. Or at least, that was when I decided to pay attention to the person he really was. Too bad I still loved him, anyway.

To think I spent almost four years after that, making excuses for his passive-aggressive comments and gaslighting, spiraling, growing needier by the day just to make sure he still needed *me*.

Rose called me out on it, though, eventually. My twin, as connected as she can be considering we're fraternal twins, not identical, saw the gradual decline, the way my light was dimming. She helped me get out. I have to remind myself frequently that I'm in a good place right now, a place where I don't need anyone. I'm in a happy place, a very fun place. Or at least I was. I still would be, if I wasn't accidentally expecting.

Theo gets the coffees, and I force myself not to pull my phone out while he's gone. He's talking to another nurse from another department, letting her go ahead of him in the line, giving her one of those heart-stopping all-white smiles. The nurse laughs, and damn if my own heart doesn't do a traitorous little flutter. Platonic or not, Theo shines most when he's being his real self, which is kind, considerate, attentive… Okay, fine, I like when his attention is on me. He's not a threat with it, like Grayson was.

Theo used to think he could flirt with me, but it doesn't work, and it never did. I don't date players. Just random, sexy Miami locals who pick me up over cocktails on SoBe and take me home on the back of an impressive, shiny red Indian Chief Vintage, apparently. If only we'd stopped on the villa's driveway. If only I hadn't invited him in.

"Nice work with that little one, Carter. He's going to be fine, I hope?" he says when he sits down, placing my coffee in front of me. I tell him of course he'll be fine, and realize I still don't really want to drink any coffee, but I bump my cup to his, tell him he was a hero as usual and take a sip so as not to seem off. I get another weird flutter when I picture that last baby's face. It didn't seem like just another doctor-patient case; it felt like something else entirely, knowing what I know. I thought about the mother even more the whole time; how was she feeling? How is she now? I'll go check on her, right after this, I decide.

"So, tell me about last night."

I know that's why Theo wanted to get me here. He wants to tell me about his date. His first with some graduate student he met in Whole Foods shopping for avocados. His regular routine. I don't know how he doesn't get tired, going on so many first dates that never amount to anything.

He rakes at his hair and launches into how he booked them into some fancy steak restaurant, only to learn she was vegan, and that apparently she was annoyed at him because she swore she told him she was vegan in the vegetable aisle and he's *clearly* just another man who doesn't listen. I tell him maybe she's right, and he continues defending himself, which would usually make me laugh.

"Are you sure you're okay? You look different," he observes. My blood spikes as his tone shifts from playful to concerned again in a blink, as is his style.

"You just keep getting more charming," I tell him. I know I must look like I'm about to burst with the weight of what I know, but how can I explain this mind-blowing maelstrom of emotions about my surprise pregnancy when I haven't even begun to understand them myself?

Before Theo can press further, a familiar figure appears in my peripheral vision. Rose, my decidedly un-pregnant twin sister, is the picture of professional poise in her equally well-ironed white coat.

"Excuse me, Dr Montgomery, can I borrow Lily for a moment?" she interjects smoothly.

"Please, take her away," he says, and I roll my eyes at him.

My beloved Rose's green eyes, exactly like mine, save for one tiny brown freckle on the perimeter of her right iris, look between us quickly, before she beckons me to follow her. I am fully expecting my twin to either reveal she knows via the Spidey line that something's amiss, or to relay the information that she'll be working late again tonight and can *I* make sure to feed our cat, Jasper. There's always some excuse to stay late in the fertility department. After four years of training in OB-GYN, she's all but been glued to her desk since going for the board certification in reproductive endocrinology and infertility. I'm proud of her of course; she needed something to get stuck into after the divorce. Even if a career as an endocrinologist puts her even more amongst women who are trying to get pregnant, women who unwittingly remind her that she was trying for a baby with David, before their marriage fell apart. I'm amazed by her strength sometimes. You'd never know she's deeply scarred underneath it.

She loops her arm through mine. Her touch is instantly grounding as she steers me away. I'm grateful for her impeccable timing, even as my stomach leaps in somersaults. *I have to tell her* is all I can think as she talks at me.

"So, Lils, we need to talk about Dad's party. Walk with me to the parking lot. I left something in the car…"

I knew it. I knew she was grabbing me while she could. Rose is always on the go; she barely gives herself time to breathe. Not that it matters if she's working late again. Tonight I'll curl up on the couch with Jasper and together we will go over this text message to *Miami Motorhead*. What was his real name? Something like Antonio? Anthony? Yes, Anthony, I think. It's so awful that I can't even remember but I wasn't supposed to ever have to think about him again. I was testing myself like I have done since it ended with Grayson, to see if I could do "casual," to see if I could come off as something other than needy.

I glance back. Theo is watching us leave. His brow is all furrowed in suspicion and something else. Annoyance? Not at Rose; he adores Rose. He just senses that I'm keeping something from him. If Grayson ever suspected I was keeping something from him, there would be hell to pay— Why can't I stop comparing everyone to him, even now?

I follow Rose down the corridor and out into the rain-drenched forecourt. The trees blow wet droplets straight onto our heads as we make our way toward the parking lot. Should I tell her now? No. It would ruin her day. She's got enough going on. I'll wait, I decide, shoving down the little voice that pipes up, calling me a coward. I *have* to trust myself with this. I'll tell *Miami Motorhead* first, and then I'll tell everyone else.

CHAPTER TWO

THE SIZZLE OF bacon fills the kitchen. I try to mimic Rose's perfected method of egg poaching, but my hands are clumsy around the pan and bits of pink shell float around the whites as I break one. I'm distracted. Jasper winds around my ankles with an insistent purr, and I absentmindedly reach down to offer him a bit of bacon. Rose appears then, tutting, and tells me cats aren't supposed to eat bacon. I disagree. I think every being on earth is supposed to eat bacon, but I don't say it because she already knows what an advocate I am for the carnivore club. Theo and I try every new steak place in town the first week they open.

"Can you believe Dad's really turning sixty next weekend?" Rose says, tutting again at the broken eggshell as she leans over my shoulder. I shrug her off and she sticks out her tongue, grabbing the ketchup from the cupboard and placing it down with a plonk on the table. My heart's beating wildly as the words build up in my throat. There are so many ways I could say it now she's awake, now that it's the weekend and we've space and time. "We need to make sure everything is perfect. The catering, the guest list, especially the—"

"Rose." My voice cuts through her party-planning monologue, sharper than I intend it to. It surprises even me, but I just can't keep this secret from her any longer.

She jolts her head up. Her eyes narrow as she studies me and tightens the belt around her plush white robe. "Do you think I picked the wrong caterer? I woke up worried about that. There's a place that does a great crawfish boil we could go with, if the Italian buffet thing is too much."

"Nothing's wrong, but...don't go for the crawfish," I say quickly. Just the thought of it turns my stomach. I've never particularly been a fan of seafood at the best of times.

"Then what is it?" She fills her coffee cup, then looks at me over it, her twin intuition on high alert. "Grayson didn't try to contact you again, did he?"

"It's not Grayson." I take a deep breath and rest my lower back against the counter, facing her. My arms feel too big in my matching robe as I fiddle with the sleeves. It's taken days for me to find the courage for this conversation, and now the words feel like boulders in my throat. "I'm pregnant."

The coffee cup she's holding clatters onto the floor. Jasper jumps in fright. She launches for a cloth and starts dragging it across the wet floor with one foot. "Jeez, Lily. You could have waited till I was sitting down!"

"What am I going to do?" I cross the kitchen and sink into the chair at the table. I feel suddenly devoid of strength. "I haven't heard back from him yet—the father. I've been waiting, giving him a chance to reply. That's why I didn't tell you sooner. I'm sorry, don't be mad."

"Mad?" Rose sinks into the chair opposite me and rakes her fingertips through her hair. She always has good hair, even when she wakes up, that silky dark mass of mahogany waves that mirrors my own. Except she keeps hers longer. I got mine trimmed to chin length before my solo vacation—the one that went so wrong. "Is it Theo's?" she asks me, and I snort.

"*Theo's?* Why would it be his?"

Rose looks confused, but mostly concerned now. She grasps my hand, knocking the ketchup over, and makes a big thing of looking very forcefully into my eyes. "I just assumed, I'm sorry, it's okay. Everything will be okay," she says, and I nod because I believe her; I have to. "How far along are you?"

"I was two weeks late," I murmur, tracing the wood grain of the tabletop. "I took three tests. Same results every time. So, about seven weeks."

I shake my head guiltily and she growls from the back of her throat, before seemingly remembering her lifetime role as my rock and squeezing my hand. "Lily, we'll figure this out. Together, all right?" She steps over what's left of the coffee spill and refills another mug. I see her staring out the window a second, and I know she's doing the math.

"So, seven weeks…"

"Miami," I blurt out. "The vacation you couldn't make because of work?"

"The *Miami Motorhead*? Oh, Lily, don't tell me… Wait, he still hasn't responded? When did you tell him?"

"On Tuesday."

"And today is Saturday—what a piece of…"

"Maybe he didn't get it for some reason," I interject as the implications start to swirl. I'm going to be a single mother. Either that or I abort; the thought has crossed my mind, of course, but it just doesn't sit right. I work around mothers and babies all day. I see how their arrivals, and sometimes premature departures, affect everyone involved. I know the likely state of my baby at any given moment. I can't unsee what I can't even see yet inside me.

My baby's brain has already started to develop; their facial features are starting to form. Rose reminds me we have a no-relationship pact, have done since we bought the house following her divorce and my…well, my disaster of a thing with Grayson, but I remind her that because of Grayson, this could be the only chance to be a mom I'll ever get.

"I never thought I'd be able to do this, because I'll probably never *have* another relationship, Rose."

She tuts again. "You're so dramatic!"

"I'm deadly serious. Men cannot be trusted! And now, well, look, no man! Just a baby, like I wanted. Maybe in a funny way, this happening now is fate."

She listens as I talk to her like always, but I know she's concerned for me, and I know she doesn't think it's funny. She sits back and sighs while Jasper leaps at a shadow. "You wanted adventure and fun after Grayson, Lils. But this…"

"I know," I mutter, thinking of the warm, muggy Florida night that started with cocktails and ended with sunrise out by the swimming pool. The luxury villa I was supposed to be sharing with Rose. A night of wild abandon with a man I assumed I'd never have anything to do with ever again. I was trying to live like Theo does. Maybe in a way I've always been a little jealous that Theo can live like every day and conquest could be his last. I've never been like that; I love too hard. I live too carefully. Not as carefully as Rose, mind you. Rose hasn't even been on a date since her eight-year marriage to David blew up. Sometimes I think watching the struggle I had with Grayson on top of all that put her off relationships for good, too, hence our pact.

She talks to me as she goes to the stove, retrieves the solidly poached and likely inedible eggs, instructs me on who I need to contact, what I need to eat. She tells me what my options are, as if I haven't already lived a lifetime's worth of research in a neonatal unit.

"The most important thing to know is that you won't be alone, Lily. You have me, and Dad and your friends..."

"Theo can't know," I say quickly, too quickly. "Not yet. He'd worry about me at work, and I can't—"

Rose narrows her eyes. "Is this why you just canceled on him for this afternoon?"

I pull a face. So she heard me on the phone before she came downstairs. I called him, canceling our regular biweekly Saturday plan to watch the NFL live in the Irish bar on Clark Street. Theo likes to pretend to watch the Chicago Bears while checking out hot tourists, and

I actually enjoy watching the football. Just not today. I couldn't face it. Or him. How can I look into his eyes and not tell him what's going on?

Rose seems to read my thought pattern as usual. "Why don't you really want to tell him?"

"Because…" I trail off, searching for the words. In truth, I know I have to tell him. And I will. But now that the coast is clear for me to do so, I just don't want him to judge me…like Grayson did.

Rose cocks her head. "You're going to have to tell him eventually, especially if you're keeping it."

She's right. There's no way out of this. He's been looking at me funny all week in the hospital, analyzing me silently behind those blue eyes. I know him. Well, I know when he's troubled. I see it a lot after he takes phone calls sometimes, whatever that's about. It always sparks a twinge of empathy somehow, like I'm pulled to a certain darkness in him as much as I'm drawn to his light.

"I don't know how to tell him," I say aloud. Why am I getting so emotional about this?

Rose picks up Jasper and snuggles into him. "We'll figure it out, don't worry. But as for everyone else…it's probably best if we keep this to ourselves until you decide what to do. We need to find you a doctor who isn't a friend or colleague," she says, getting back to her eggs. "Someone discreet. I'll arrange it."

"Thank you," I whisper. What would I ever do without my sister?

"Code blue!" The intercom shatters whatever was left of my early Monday morning calm as I sprint down the hallway from the elevator, my scrubs rustling, my sneakers squeaking. I burst into the ER. Theo's already here, his hands moving deftly, his face a picture of determination as he intubates a tiny infant and informs me quickly of the situation while I pull on my gloves. I have to force my mind to transition from calm to emergency mode. I was just upstairs in the NICU with Zara, the young mother of the baby we helped last week. The one she's since named Tomas. We've kept them in for observation but they should both be released today.

"Bag ready, Doctor Montgomery?" I keep my voice calm as I take over, and he keeps his blue eyes laser focused. His gloves squeak against mine as he takes it and I feel a momentary jolt to my lower intestines as my secret rattles around inside me.

"Good. Keep an eye on his sats," I instruct, referring to the baby's oxygen saturation levels. This little mite has been having trouble breathing on his own since he was born in a car several blocks away, gridlocked in traffic, only twenty-three minutes ago. I try not to let the nausea I've felt all morning affect me as I watch the monitors like a hawk and report the numbers out loud. My mind is whirring with its own countdown toward my scan tomorrow. We booked it at Dawson's Clinic, just out of town, so no one here has to do it. Rose will come with me, of course.

"Come on, little guy," I murmur to the baby, and Theo looks away just as I pull my hand from my lower belly, where it seems to keep moving to all on its own. "His sats are picking up," I announce, clearing my throat, ignoring the look he's giving me. I'll tell him I've got a stomach-ache if he asks. But lying won't work; he's not an idiot. Look at where he works. He's going to see right through me.

The baby's breathing stabilizes. Soon, the whirlwind of activity around me reduces to just Theo and me. He yanks off his gloves and throws them into the wastebasket across the room, as I tell Amber to bring the baby's mother in from where she's waiting right outside in a wheelchair. She needs to go to the maternity ward, and I need to finish my rounds in the NICU, where this little one belongs, too, for the meantime.

I watch the young woman's face as she strokes her little boy's cheek around the tubes. Her baby's eyelashes are fluttering, his puckered little face exploring new expressions. My eyes are starting to leak at the corners and people are going to see. I tell Amber I'll see them upstairs and try not to look back over my shoulder at Theo. He's still watching me. I can feel it. I should take him aside on the next break and tell him, just come right out and say it. But I'm scared, no thanks to Grayson.

Far from the caring man I fell in love with in the early days, the one who was careful to remain the considerate partner so I wouldn't see through the veneer, toward the end of our relationship Grayson became someone I lived in fear of telling anything to that might alter his opinion of me further. The abuse was subtle at first, barbs and jabs inflicted with a smile or a cocked eyebrow. He would lure me to the bedroom with compliments and love bombs, then berate me for wearing the wrong color underwear, and then try to sleep with me, anyway. He'd praise my cooking, then refuse to eat it. If I asked why, he'd say he was sure it didn't taste as good as it looked, leaving me alone in silence and confusion, to box it up and bring it over to my sister.

Theo isn't Grayson, not at all, but he'll start to look at me as something broken, someone who made a terrible mistake, someone who's the opposite of everything he thought I was.

I catch myself. Theo's my friend, and this is

my business. Isn't it his duty to support me? Why do I care so much what Theo thinks these days, just because those bright blue eyes might see more than I ever realized?

The last patient has been wheeled away and the weight of the longest Monday on record is a kettlebell on my shoulders as I fumble for my car keys in the parking lot. I'm almost at my car when I hear his familiar baritone behind me.

"Carter!" He jogs lightly to catch up with me. "You left before I could catch you…"

My fingers clasp around my keys in the bottom of my purse and I pull them out, turning to face him slowly. "What's up?" I say, avoiding his gaze.

"Come on… Really? *What's up?* We're really going to do this?" His tone is gentle but probing as he takes a step closer. "You bailed on our game date on Saturday. Since when do you turn down a chance to gloat over a bucket of wings?"

"That's your idea of a *date*, Theo? Hearing a woman gloat over fried chicken?"

"Depends what she's done to gloat about," he says with a smirk, and I raise my eyes to the roof.

"Oh, come on, Lily." He scowls at me till his brows touch, which somehow still makes him look impossibly handsome. "You're being weird."

"It's just a busy time, Theo... Dad's party and all that."

His blue eyes cloud momentarily. Hurt flickers across his face, and I hate how it lashes at my heart like a whip. He doesn't know Rose's words got to me more than they should have over the weekend; did she actually think this baby could be Theo's? She knows Theo and I have never been more than friends and colleagues. I guess there might have been a time when his advances were kind of tempting, once I'd moved into the house with Rose and was starting to feel more like myself again. But by then we were firmly in the friendship zone—a fling would have messed it up. And it's not like Theo ever wants more than a fling.

"Actually, speaking of dates, I canceled one myself this weekend," he says now, eyeing me down his nose. Looking down his nose at me is not unusual, seeing as he's six foot four.

"Did you?" I ask, genuinely surprised. "Losing your touch?"

"Hardly," he shoots back with a grin that doesn't quite reach his eyes. It roots me to the spot. "I just had other things on my mind."

We stand facing each other. The space between us charges by the second with a thousand unspoken words and a truckload of tension I'm not ready to unpack.

Tell him, my brain screeches at me. *Why can't you just say it?*

Unless he knows somehow. Is he testing me? Waiting for me to say it first?

"Changing the subject," he says after a beat. "Need me to whip up a batch of my chili chocolate cupcakes for Geoff's party?"

"Your what?" I laugh despite myself. For a second there, I really thought he was going to tell me he knew about the baby somehow. "You mean the ones that sent Verity Henderson into a coughing fit last Christmas? She almost redecorated Dad's kitchen in a *very* disturbing shade of brown after eating *half* of one."

"Purely coincidental," Theo insists with mock indignation. "I'll have you know those are a surefire win at every baking contest I enter."

"Only because they're too afraid to disqualify you," I tease. "In case they ever need you in an emergency of some kind."

Theo winces, placing a hand over his heart. "You wound me, Carter."

"Get a bandage," I say before reminding him that I know for a fact he's never entered any baking contests in his life.

"You underestimate me," he says. "If you knew even half of my talents, you'd be nothing short of intimidated."

"Intimidated? I've seen puppies more intimidating than you. You're just a prize-winning flirt, that's what you are."

His snort, which morphs into a chuckle, tells me he's enjoying our banter as much as I am, but for some reason I'm reading more into what he means by *talents* than I usually would, and now I'm thinking about what he really must be like in the bedroom. Damn Rose, getting in my head.

I unlock my car with a beep. "Just make sure those *talents* don't include food poisoning half the party guests," I tell him.

"So, that means I'm coming. With cakes."

"Affirmative," I say with a smile.

His tone softens suddenly, then turns serious, and my stomach twists. "Listen, Carter, if there's anything else—"

"I know where to find you," I finish for him, sliding into the driver's seat. I close the door on him and he crosses his arms. That serious expression on his face is gnawing at me more by the second. I'm a coward, I know I am, and if I keep this from him much longer, only for him to find out, it won't be great for our friendship. But I can't have this bond turned on its head just yet. It means too much to me.

CHAPTER THREE

I'M TALKING TO myself under my breath, deep house music blasting from my stereo. My egg whites are being whisked with a bit more vigor than is probably necessary, too. The recipe called for something like "a delicate hand," but I'll leave that to the ER. My mind isn't really focused on the fluffiness of egg whites right now. It's on Lily's latest bout of uncharacteristic silence. I didn't even bother pushing her this time; I know she hates that. And I didn't want to hear her brush me off again.

I take the bowl over to the windows and rest my eyes on the green of the trees, the two pigeons in their usual spot. My corner of Winnetka looks pretty shiny beyond the terrace this morning, shinier than I feel, considering it's Saturday and I have to be at her dad's birthday party this afternoon. I *was* looking forward to it. Lily's family is great. Usually, I invite myself over before they get a chance to; they're everything my own family is not. But something's very off with Lily. I would rather just hit the home gym again than probe and press her on it, only to be rebuffed.

Still, I made a promise. I'm already on my third batch of chili chocolate cupcakes when Taylor Swift blasts out around the room, cutting through my thoughts. My hands are still covered in cocoa powder as I fumble for my cell. My sister. "Peonie. Are you aware your daughter changed my ringtone to Taylor Swift again?"

"You shouldn't leave your phone unlocked, Theo." Peonie's voice is too energetic for the hour. She's probably been to yoga class, walked the dog and dropped Delilah off at the stables for her horse-riding lesson already. She's the mother she always wanted to be, the woman our own mother never was…and still isn't.

I brace myself for Pea to tell me what Mom's done now. It was her turn to welcome the new carer, a sweet lady called Edwina. Let's just hope this one sticks.

Whenever I think about our bipolar, alcohol-addicted mother it's a one-way ticket back to the pits of hell that constituted my childhood. Her demons succeed in every situation; even her psychologist is afraid of her. She's struggled with addiction our entire lives but as kids, Pea and I lived in complete fear of her erratic behavior, her crying fits, her bouts of rage. Oh, she'd be kind, too. She'd gush over us, tell everyone around how wonderful we were, get our hopes up. Then before we knew it, she'd be yelling and sobbing and telling us she should never have had us.

She targeted Dad a lot, until he had enough and divorced her. It's had all manner of repercussions on Pea and me over the years, but I don't talk about those any more than Pea does. She's got her family. I've got my work. All we can do is love our mother, ensure the carers who come into her home are the best we can afford, even if she detests all of them, and let her spend time with Delilah. My niece is literally the only person she tolerates.

"To what do I owe this pleasure? I'm kinda busy," I tell her. She snorts.

"Oh, really? How many women are you juggling this morning, darling brother? Cooking breakfast for one before you head out to meet another for brunch, am I right?"

I don't even bother to defend myself. I *was* a player. I mean, I *have* been, but I've canceled more dates than I've shown up to lately. It's all just getting a little tiring, especially with things how they are at work.

And with Lily, drifting away from me.

I've considered that maybe she's bored of me, but we've never been bored together ever; we have too much stupid banter going between us for that. I've been watching her. I'm pretty sure I know what I'm looking at. I just hope to God I'm wrong.

I tell Pea she's deranged and we play-bicker like we normally do for a moment before she finally gets back to what I knew was coming the second she called.

"So, Mom," Pea sighs, I can almost see her rubbing her temples as I check on my latest batch of cakes. They're browning nicely. "You know she's off the meds again."

I knew it. "Great news, just great," I say through my teeth. Same old story. It doesn't take much for my brain to serve a throwback to a million situations I had to all but drag Pea away from when she was a kid. When *I* was still a kid. I can hardly blame Dad for taking off, but no one wants to think they were abandoned, and I've tried to make it up to Pea her whole life.

Me…well, I just abandon people before they can jump ship themselves. Rip the bandage off for minimal pain all around. Isn't that how you do it?

Pea continues. "Before Edwina arrived today she locked herself in the bathroom to count the wall tiles again. Edwina is saying she's refusing the pills. She spat them out and tried to stuff them down the sofa."

I glance at my newest batch of unfinished cupcakes. We found a whole pharmacy's worth of pills down the sofa last time we checked. "All right, I'll talk to her after Geoff's party."

Pea tells me thanks and excuses herself to get back to watching Delilah practice her show-jumps. They say she's pretty advanced for an eleven-year-old. Delilah is somewhat of a child prodigy, although we might be biased. She's the best thing to happen to our family for a long time, and the one thing that gives Pea hope that Mom might change, someday. If it wasn't for how nice Mom is with Dee, and how soft Pea is, she'd probably be in rehab already.

I shower and change, box up my cakes and make my way to the party. Pea's in my head the whole time. She didn't see the half of what I did growing up. Being six years older than her, I did everything to protect her from Mom's disease. I whisked her off to our late Granny Fran whenever I could, and I thank whatever God is up there that Granny Fran took us in after Dad left and Mom stopped working and we lost the house. I know Pea is scarred like I am. But she's also an infuriating optimist. She married her high-school sweetheart, Riley, when she was twenty, popped Delilah out just eight months later, and to this day she continues trying to be everything she can be for her daughter. She does her best to give her everything *she* never had, and still never gets from Mom.

If I have to deal with more of Mom's drama just to keep Pea happy, of course I will, but if things get worse I'll have no choice but to put her in rehab.

I frown, even as I walk up the driveway. It's not just Mom I have to worry about now. Lily's not the same lately; she's hiding something. She's definitely hiding something, and I think I know what it is. And I don't like it one little bit.

The door swings open before I can knock. Animated chatter floods my ears. The twins' place is a remodeled tenement, and its Glenview bones are at least a hundred years older than the modern furniture they filled it with when they bought it together. They got it after Rose's divorce. I think Lily's last long-term relationship fell apart sometime before that, though she doesn't say much about that—some guy called Grayson, whom she never seems to want to talk about. I don't push it. She and I met after that ended anyway, the first day she started at Evergreen, when I hit on her, of course; she's hot. She shut me down, quite rightly. So I took what I could, which was her friendship, even though we have a connection.

More than just a connection, if I'm honest with

myself. She's fun, and smart and beautiful and thoughtful and kind, but I'm drawn to her for other reasons I can't explain, and I guess that's why I respect her boundaries. If I tried anything on now, it would ruin this comfy thing we've built, and it means too much to me at this point.

"Theo, hi." Rose greets me with her usual efficiency, taking the cupcakes and barely pausing for air as she whisks them away and tells me Lily is in the kitchen with Geoff.

I move through the throng of guests. My presence elicits a mix of polite nods and less subtle, appreciative glances from women I barely recognize. But as always, it's Lily's reaction I find myself seeking out. These past few days, I haven't known which reaction I'm likely to get. It's like she's become increasingly elusive with every passing day.

"Doctor Theo Montgomery!" Lily's father, Geoff is calling out from across the room, using my full title as usual. Lily is next to him, at the far end of the dinner table, nestled between cousins I've met maybe once or twice. Geoff gets up to greet me. Lily does not. She offers a faded smile as her dad and I do our usual high five that blends into a fist bump. Geoff thinks it's cool. I don't like to make him think it's not.

She touches her hair as Geoff tells me for the hundredth time what a great job he's heard I'm doing at Evergreen, and also that he knows I won my last boxing match. Did Lily tell him that? Through the window, I can see Jasper, the world's most pampered British shorthair, lounging on a pillowy shelf in his cattery. I don't like cats, never have. I think it goes back to Granny Fran's second husband always moaning about their cat's hair everywhere, then finding some in my cornflakes.

I feel Lily's green gaze on me the whole time, but I don't go over to her. I can almost feel how she doesn't want me to, which is what's eating at me. I want to at least know she's okay.

I'm swept around the room by everyone from Geoff's lawyer to Rose's hairdresser, but I can feel the tension radiating off Lily. It's concentrating in a tight ball between us and I know she feels it, too. She's wearing a thick cardigan over a wraparound dress. Even from here I can see her boobs are bigger. Swollen. She'd hate that I'm noticing things like this, the changing shape of her breasts, but I'm a doctor, and I'm human.

"Drink?" Rose asks me, reappearing like a ghost at my side.

"Water's fine, thanks." My gaze drifts back to Lily. She seems to be wilting like a flower left too long in the sun. I really hope my suspicions aren't correct, but she's also only drinking water.

"Make sure he eats something," I hear one of

the aunts say about me, fussing over my plate like I am still a teenager. It's true. I've only taken a couple of small items from the Italian buffet catering that's spread about in trays on the counters. This isn't like me. Food is our thing, but Pea got to me, and Lily's getting to me, too.

"Trust me, Aunt Carol, I can fend for myself," I say, anyway, adding a wink I know she'll appreciate, and she pats my cheek fondly.

I get a sudden flashback to being eight, or nine, asking Mom if I could have a bag of chips, only for her to make me separate them on a plate into different size categories. Pea was a toddler. She grabbed a chip from my plate, as toddlers do, and Mom flew into a rage about how no one appreciates her when she tries to teach us discipline.

I couldn't fend for myself for a long time. Everything I had I gave to Pea. And nothing I ever did was appreciated, not by our mother, anyway. I guess if you were to psychoanalyze me you'd say that was why I went all out in a profession where I'd always be useful and always be rewarded for it. ER doctors don't get abandoned. We're essential workers; we're necessary. My eyes are drawn back to Lily as she stands abruptly, her chair scraping against the hardwood floor. Her hand flies to her mouth, eyes wide with panic.

"Excuse me," she mumbles. Then she makes a dash for the bathroom. The room goes quiet.

"Rose, I'll go—" I start, already stepping forward.

"Theo, it's okay. I've got her," Rose interrupts. Her calmness would be fully convincing to most people, but it's her eyes that betray her. She's worried, and not just because Lily is her sister.

"Let me check on her," I insist. I'm an ER doctor; I am usually untouchable. So why is my heart flapping like a trapped bird right now?

"Fine," Rose concedes. She follows just a step behind as I push through the hallway and find Lily leaning against the cool tile of the bathroom wall. Her face is ashen.

"Leave us please," I tell Rose, and she cocks her eyebrow at me in suspicion as I shut the door, locking us in.

"What's going on?" I kneel beside her. "Carter, talk to me. You're greener than the Hulk."

"I'm fine," she lies, her breathing shallow. She meets my eyes, then looks away. My hand finds hers before I sweep her cheek. She's hot in my hand, clammy, and she starts peeling off her cardigan while I fill a glass with water.

"You don't look fine."

"Can we just…not do this here?" Her voice cracks as she takes the glass and downs three huge mouthfuls.

"Are you pregnant, Lily?"

The question hangs in the air like a charged particle. I watch the shock ribbon out across her green eyes, eyes that I've fallen into more times than I care to admit when we've been out talking, in bars, downing shots at the end of crazy shifts. She puts the water down too heavily on the floor. I drop to my haunches again and she covers her face.

"Theo, how could you even—"

"You think I haven't noticed? The way your clothes are fitting differently, the way you're so tired all the time lately… It's written all over your face, every shift."

She sinks back against the bathroom wall as if my words are a physical blow, her hands fluttering to her stomach protectively. I still feel hotter than I should, knowing this is what she's been hiding from me. Why was she hiding it from me? Doesn't she trust me?

"I—I don't know what to say."

"Start with the truth," I instruct.

"Eight weeks," she murmurs. She's barely audible above the noise of my own heart in my ears. "I'm eight weeks along."

"Eight weeks," I echo numbly. I mean, I had an inkling, but now that she's confirming it I can't process any of this.

"And before you ask," she continues, "the father doesn't want anything to do with me. Or the baby. He's in Miami."

Anger flares within me, fierce and protective. A kind I haven't felt for a long time, the kind that makes me grapple for control. Lily sees it bubbling and her hand on my arm stops me cold. "I'm okay with it. I don't need him. I have Rose," she says.

I have so many questions, but I'm having to rein in my temper. This isn't about me. It's about Lily, about supporting her, no matter how much this situation makes my blood boil. If he's in Miami, this happened on that trip she took. She even told me about the guy afterward, the hookup at the villa. I think I even laughed and told her *Well done*. Right before I stood alone at the bar for ten minutes on my phone, so I wouldn't have to look at her and picture another guy all over her.

Not important. None of that is important.

"Well, now I know, Lily." I wait until her gaze meets mine again. "I'm with you, all right? Whether you decide to keep it or not."

Her eyes narrow in a flash of annoyance. "Why wouldn't I keep it? It's not like I'll ever get another chance."

I ask her what she means; she has plenty of time to meet someone and have a family if that's what she wants, but she looks sideways and mumbles something about Grayson.

"What about Grayson?"

"I just don't want another relationship, Theo. Can we leave it please?"

I shut my mouth. I know better than to offer my opinion here; it's not like I'm the father. But what the hell does her ex-boyfriend have to do with this situation, or her not wanting another relationship? What did Grayson do?

"Nobody else knows except Rose yet," she says, stopping my thoughts in their tracks. "I'll tell them today. I'll tell Dad."

"Damn it, Lily." The words blurt out with more emotion than I mean for her to hear as I sink to the floor against the wall beside her. "Why didn't you say anything to me sooner?"

"Because I was scared, Theo."

"Of what? Of me?"

"Of everything changing."

The way she says it pushes a mute button in me. I clamp my lips shut. I almost can't process what it is I'm actually feeling, but everything *did* just change. She won't need me around for much longer, not in the same way, and a prickly heat floods my veins at the thought of being shut out. A regression to a million memories of being told I'm not enough. It's my fault, not Lily's, but still, we just became two very different people.

CHAPTER FOUR

Eight weeks later

IT'S SO PEACEFUL and quiet in Neonatal this rainy late-September morning, save for the regular beeps and murmurs. I navigate the rows of incubators that each house a fragile new life and as usual, I think about the life inside me. He, or she, is making their presence known a little more each day beneath my scrubs.

I kind of like the gentle but insistent pressure against my waistband. I like the fact that my miracle skin is stretching to accommodate new life. It's almost time to get new clothes. I haven't gotten around to it yet. I know Rose is too busy to make it a priority and I guess I'm not pushing it because, like with a lot of the smaller activities that no one else thinks twice about, shopping was ruined for me once. I think about this one incident with Grayson every time I'm in a clothing store. He told me I looked beautiful in a dress I wanted to wear for a wedding. I was buzzing. Finally, a compliment! Then, when the assistant left, he told me I was dreaming if I thought he'd ever let me wear something so revealing and trashy in public.

But sixteen weeks in and I'm starting to show now. It's quite amazing. Terrifying, too.

"Morning, Ezra," I whisper to a preemie girl with a fuzz of chestnut hair. She's just waking up, her face all cutely scrunched. "How are you doing today?"

All through my rounds, my mind wanders to the little being inside me. Is it dreaming? Can it sense the love already enveloping it from this side of the world? Rose, Dad, and my aunt and Theo, too, all think I'm crazy for going into this alone, not that they're telling me. Theo's been keeping his respectful distance. I think he's weirded out by it all. I've been telling myself he'll come around, and I hope he does because I'm starting to miss him. But I don't *need* him, or anyone. I'm doing this alone by choice. I have to keep reminding myself of that.

"Looks like someone's popped," comes a soft voice. I look up into the eyes of Sheena. Her son Vivek has been fighting valiantly ever since his premature arrival three weeks ago. She's always the first in when I open the doors for visits.

"Is it that obvious?" I ask. I can feel my cheeks

warming as I say it. A little pride, a little embarrassment, I suppose.

Sheena throws me a knowing smile. "Only to a practiced eye." She reaches out, her fingertips hovering but not touching my midsection. "You've got that glow, Doctor Carter. And I don't just mean the pregnant one—you always have a shine about you."

This is news to me. I saw myself as a shell for a long time, even after I left Grayson. In a way, Theo brought me out of myself. When we met, one of the reasons I was drawn to him was because he made me laugh. I already miss that.

Sheena touches Vivek's incubator. "He's been gaining weight, hasn't he?"

"Yep. He's a fighter," I affirm, watching as she strokes the back of Vivek's tiny hand with her fingertip. The baby has tubes aiding his breathing and feeding but he clenches reflexively. His miniature grip is strong. A very good sign. Sheena tells me she was so grateful when I explained the PDA ligation, even before the surgeon came to speak to her. She's referring to the procedure performed to correct her son's heart complication. "You were amazing, keeping me calm, explaining everything... I felt beyond lost."

She asks if I've picked out names yet, or if I'm waiting to find out the sex, and the question hangs in the air as I secure a blanket around another newborn. "Actually, I'm having the scan this afternoon," I admit. "At another facility."

Just as I say it, a shadow falls across the medical chart in my hands.

"This afternoon?" I look up. Theo's here. He's popped up on his break, like he does sometimes, not that he's done it a lot lately, though. A pang hits my heart like a ping from a rubber band. I've missed him. Maybe more than I thought.

Sheena makes her exit and he leans casually against the door frame. His coat is ironed to perfection as usual but he looks a little tired. I clutch the chart like a shield, then press a hand absently to my belly. "Sneaking up on me, are you?"

"Stealth is part of the job description," he says. I give him some flippant comeback, but I can't help but wonder if he's been out all night on a hot date, and a bolt of something like jealousy rocks me from my sneakers up to my throat. Why is my brain trying to trick me? Hormones, probably. Everything is out of balance. Theo's distance since Dad's party has gotten to me. He's been supportive enough around here on the brief occasions we've met, but he hasn't asked me to go to the Irish pub, or to come watch him box, or to do anything much at all out of hours, ever since. It's like he sees me as a different person, just like I feared.

"The ultrasound is this afternoon, after my shift," I tell him now.

"The big gender reveal, right?"

"Right," I echo, and there's an awkward pause as we both seem to grapple with the implications. Today it gets real. *More* real. I find out if the life I am carrying is male or female, and whether everything is developing as it should.

"Rose will be with you," he says, pulling out his phone, looking at it, then shoving it back into his pocket. He looks stressed.

"Yes. Is everything okay?" I ask.

"Mmm-hmm." He walks around the unit and doesn't elaborate, and I don't pry. I know how his mom and sister stress him out, just from seeing his face after he talks to one of them, but I don't know much beyond that. I asked once, and he shut me down. Since then I haven't probed much into his personal life beyond what he chooses to tell me. It's not like I haven't shut him down before when he's tried to talk about me and Grayson. But for some reason, probably because I have missed him, I ask him if he wants to talk about it.

He stops by an incubator and shakes his head without looking at me, and I curb the flare of annoyance from escaping my mouth. It feels like he's renouncing my right to know things about him slowly but surely, day by day. I hate feeling so powerless, but the moment stretches until it's thin enough to snap.

"Hey," I begin, fidgeting with the hem of my white coat. "I'm kind of nervous about the ultrasound today, actually. I might take the morning off tomorrow, depending on how it goes. I'll put the locum on standby."

He looks up now, crossing the space between us. "I thought you didn't do nervous, Carter. Isn't that your superpower?" His tone is lighter, but his eyes search mine with genuine concern, and a small weight lifts from my shoulders. So he does still care, which I guess is the reason I'm telling him, to see if he does. Which is kind of pathetic. He's not Grayson, so what am I doing?

"Carrying a human inside me is my superpower," I say. "Would you do it, if you could?"

"Carry a human inside me?" He seems to contemplate it for a moment, and the look on his handsome face is already making me smile. "I don't think I would, no. Delilah is enough. She keeps changing my ringtone to Taylor Swift. It's really not ideal in emergency situations."

"I've missed you," I tell him before I can order myself not to. I can't control the tears that prick at my eyes from out of nowhere, and I swipe at them in embarrassment. Grayson hated when I cried; he said I was weak. "Sorry, gosh, my hormones are all over the place. I'm a crazy person, ignore me."

He lowers his head and looks up at me from under his eyelashes. Then he grimaces. "I've upset you by backing off, haven't I?"

"Kind of," I admit. "I mean, you said and did all the right things when you found out but then you pulled a Houdini, so yeah, I guess I'm a bit confused."

He's quiet for a moment. I can tell the wheels are turning in his head. "I wasn't really sure how much you'd *want* me to be around—" He trails off and steps closer, but I cross my arms. I won't appear weak. *Miami Motorhead*, aka Anthony, finally got in touch. He said he would support my decision, but doesn't want to be involved, just like I suspected. I left it. I don't need him. I don't need anyone. At least, I don't *want* to need anyone.

"I know you've been tired, and nauseated. I didn't think you'd appreciate me trying to make extracurricular plans. I'll make it up to you," Theo says, and the regret in his voice makes me bite back a smile. "I promise to be a better friend from now on. Do you need a foot rub? Got any weird cravings I can satisfy?"

"Like what?" I ask, and he reminds me how I once dealt with a woman who'd taken to licking dry tennis balls during her second trimester. Finally, it feels like we have our old banter back. I'm about to ask him if he wants to hang out tonight when the emergency alarm goes off in the hallway, and he's forced into a sprint from the room.

The clock reads five forty-five after another hectic day. My appointment at Dawson's is in thirty minutes. I check my watch again, pulling my jacket on, looking around for Rose. We were both supposed to be taking my car and meeting here, in the parking lot.

My phone rings, and my heart makes a dash for my throat when I see her face on the screen. "Rose?"

"Sorry, sorry, sorry, sorry, forgive me," comes her stream of despair. She's been held up after the board director dropped in unannounced. He wants to take the team for dinner to discuss potential candidates for a new role they're recruiting for soon, and can we possibly please reschedule the scan for the morning?

I can hear the regret in her voice. It breaks my heart. It's not her fault the board director is so demanding, even though it feels like she's always working these days. And what if they don't have an appointment for the morning? I'm not quite ready to take my personal affairs to Evergreen where everyone knows me; telling them

I'm pregnant with a baby that the father wants nothing to do with was bad enough.

"It's more that I've been psyching myself up for this all day, and I didn't want to go alone," I tell her.

"I'm the worst sister, Lily. Forgive me."

"Where do you have to go alone? Not to your ultrasound, I hope?" Theo's deep voice makes me spin around. He's wearing that slightly worn leather jacket, the one with the sleeves a little frayed at the edges and the scuffed elbows. The white shirt he's wearing underneath is ironed perfectly, even the pocket. The look, which I'm sure he knows, screams Chicago's hottest bachelor. Even his dark jeans are crease-free. He looks like he's changed to go somewhere else, not just home. Why does this make me feel so uncomfortable?

I pull a face and tell him how Rose can't make it. Rose is still on the line. "Theo, Theo can take you, right?" she says in my ear, like she's single-handedly discovered the perfect solution. I think Theo hears her.

"Sure, I'll go with you," he offers. Then he pauses, bringing his car keys up from the depths of his pocket. "If you want me to, Carter."

I don't, actually. Until today he was distancing himself, which still annoys me more than it probably should, even though I know why. And also, attending scans is a privilege for family members and significant others. But I have neither of those today, and I really *don't* want to go alone.

We take his car. Theo's very proud of his car. He's never said it but I can tell, even though it's as sparse inside as his apartment. There isn't even a Coke can on the floor, or a book flung in the back seat. He doesn't seem to have a lot of stuff, I've noticed. I don't know why. Maybe he's as commitment phobic with stuff as he is with people.

He sends a message when we stop at the lights, but I don't see who it's for. He gets a message back, a couple, actually, but he never looks at his phone again. The Porsche's wheels hum against the pavement, a soothing lullaby that almost makes me forget the flutter of nerves in my stomach. Theo talks about the concert he's taking Delilah to. He worships his eleven-year-old niece, Delilah. I like her, too. We bonded at a museum-night sleepover a couple years back. I casually ask if everything in his family is okay again now, and he shrugs. His expression darkens for a moment but still, I don't press it. For a second he looks more nervous than I do and it hits me; I really don't know that much about Theo, and I want to.

* * *

We arrive at Dawson's at six twenty-five.

"Are you doing all right?" Theo asks me from behind the wheel. I click off my seat belt as he parks the car. He was quiet the whole drive.

"Are *you* all right?" I reply. "You seem nervous."

He sniffs. "We're finding out the sex of this baby. I'm nervous for you, Carter. What if it's an impossibly handsome boy like me who's going to cause you years of trouble?"

I huff a laugh, and he exits the car, but I know he's covering for something. I can't focus on that now, though. I'm just so grateful he's come.

The sterile halls echo with hushed voices and the occasional squeak of rubber-soled shoes as we step into the ultrasound room. I almost want to turn around again, but Theo is blocking the door, his jacket and mine draped over one arm.

"Ms. Carter?" The sonographer Dr. Priya Sharma's voice is gentle, grounding. I lie back on the examination table, the paper crinkling beneath me. Theo is still standing by the door. I bet he feels so awkward.

"You can come closer, if you like," Dr. Sharma says, and before I can tell him that he can wait outside if he wants, Theo places the jackets onto a nearby chair, steps to my side and reaches for my hand. I squeeze it, as if I can possibly transfer my racing heartbeat into his warm, steady palm.

"Are we ready to see what this little one's up to?" She starts to spread the cool gel across my abdomen. I try to steady my breathing as the monitor flickers. Dr. Sharma moves the smooth, hard tool gently around my midsection and narrows her eyes for a split second. I catch it and my stomach plummets.

Oh, no, what?

I see Theo's face next. His blue eyes widen, and he leans in closer to the screen at the exact same moment Dr. Priya does. I follow his eyes. An exhilarated smile stretches out his face, and I almost choke on my own breath.

"Twins," Theo announces, before Dr. Priya can.

She nods and lets him wheel the monitor closer so I can see better.

Twins.

The word echoes through the room, doubling itself in my mind. Twins? I turn to Theo, who's still grinning in a way that makes him look ten years younger and twenty times more handsome. Here they are, right here. Two little beings, my babies, dancing in their own private universe.

"Twins are a huge part of my family. They have been for generations, but somehow I never really thought…" My voice trails off. I'm lost in a swell of emotions now, just looking at the screen. I am completely mesmerized by what I'm seeing and soon I'm hearing it, too—two tiny hearts beating in sync.

"They're cooking along nicely, Carter," Theo says proudly.

"Would you like to know the genders?" Dr. Sharma asks. My palm is warm and clammy now from my nerves, glued to Theo's. He's still mouthing the word *twins* to himself, and there's a look of disbelief and wonderment on his face that I've never actually seen before. Am I ready? I think I am. I tell her yes. I think I'm feeding off Theo's excitement.

Dr. Sharma begins with another swirl of the cool wand over my abdomen. "You're having a boy and a girl."

"One of each, no…" Theo lets out a laugh, just as I do.

A boy and a girl. This is crazy. More tears gather in the corners of my eyes. "Just like Rose dreamed," I remember suddenly. Weirdly, Rose said she had a dream the other night, in which I announced this exact thing. I wish she were here now. She'd be wrapped around their little fingers already, too.

"Congratulations, Carter," Theo whispers. I know I'm emotional, but his words tingle my ear and send a flush of adrenaline to my nerves. I can't help missing my sister, but I'm so relieved that someone's here to witness this. That *Theo* is here to witness this.

"Congratulations, *both* of you," Dr. Priya says, making me a printout so I can show Rose. She's going to be so thrilled. Just wait till she... Wait... *What did she say?*

"Oh, no," I insert as it hits me what this lady just alluded to. "Theo's not... I mean, we're not..."

"They're going to be so loved, right, wifey?" Theo finishes for me. He's still marveling at the screen. He really does look fiercely determined now and I let the comment go.

They will definitely be loved. But my friend and colleague has just been mistaken for the father of these babies, and more concerning, for a hot fleeting second there I caught myself wishing he really *were*.

CHAPTER FIVE

"DOCTOR MONTGOMERY, heart rate's dropping. Severe cord prolapse." The obstetrician's voice cuts through the cacophony of the ER. I glance at the monitor. The mother and baby just arrived five minutes ago, and her baby's heart rate is plummeting while it's being strangled by the umbilical cord. In the next room the mother's relative, or friend, is sobbing. This precious life is hanging in the balance right in front of us, tangled in its own lifeline.

"Clamp." The obstetrician's command is met with immediate action as the team rallies around us. "We need to get this baby out now."

"Prepping for episiotomy." Her hands and feet move in a blur around the gurney as she prepares for the necessary incision. "Anesthesiologist?"

"Here," Dr. Zhalo calls. I continue monitoring the fluids as he prepares to issue an epidural. The laboring woman is far too quiet. I can read the panic on her face.

Lily's just appeared. She meets my eyes as

we work, on standby to get this child up to the NICU. She looks just as anxious. Would I do this if I could? Lily asked before, so I considered it. I love Delilah to death, but my own kids... I always assumed that whole "being a dad" thing was off the cards, seeing as I've never entertained a long-term commitment.

I doubt I could offer them any more stability at this point in my life than my own mother could when I was a kid, but I'm thirty-eight. A man at least has to think about these things. There was a weird moment in that ultrasound room the other week when I caught myself pretending those twins were mine, and I actually felt excited. I pictured me and Lily, too, for a moment, doing things parents do, and I didn't feel the pang of fear that would usually force thoughts like that away. Maybe that was why I took her shopping the other day, even if we only managed to hit one store. She doesn't know my past, but she always did make the future feel more bearable, whatever it might have in store.

Why can't I get Carter out of my head?

The room becomes a flurry of sterile blues. We do our best to provide all the comfort this woman needs. Lily is still on standby and I wonder what's going round in that mind of hers. I think all the time about how pregnancy must be changing her perspective on her job here, as well as her body. Her boobs are huge now. Her midsection is swollen, taut. She still looked pretty hot in that floaty dress I insisted I buy for her. She looked embarrassed, and I tried not to notice how charged the air was between us in that tiny changing room, when I did up the zipper. How my stomach clenched every time I pictured her with the guy who put those babies inside her.

"She's ready for arrival," someone calls. I take over the machines again while they work at carefully guiding the baby out. The cord is wound around the baby's neck like a vine, but soon a shrill cry tells us we're out of the woods. A regular slippery, squirming, perfect infant is going to live to take another breath, and hopefully many more after that.

"Welcome to the world," Lily murmurs. I watch her swaddle the child and tell us they'll take it to the NICU for further monitoring, just to be sure. She gives me a weary smile, and all I think is how I want to swaddle *her* and protect *her*, not that it's my duty to. I mean, it's none of my business if she wants to do this alone, but it's not going to be easy for her. She'll always have me, though. I realized that the second I saw those little beans sprouting limbs and cooking up faces on the ultrasound. It's not like me to get sentimental. I don't get sentimental about anything, not possessions, not people. The day we lost the house, when I was ten, Pea and I were marched out with nothing but a bag of clothes and a few toys each, and since then, I don't know... I still keep everything pretty minimal in my life. I don't "do" attachment. But Lily's part in my life is not minimal, and she isn't just anyone.

The rest of the morning is relatively quiet and my mind wanders. Usually, I'd be thinking about my last date. I forced myself to go to McFadden's with the cute blonde accountant last night—the one I canceled on at the last minute to go with Carter to her ultrasound the other week. But I bowed out early. My mind wasn't on it and she could tell. She kept on asking me if I had somewhere else to be. In the end I had to apologize and tell her I did. I drove to see Mom, who sat there accusing me of being nosy and disrespectful, while I gently reminded her that, despite those facts, she had to take her meds.

Then I drove to Carter's and parked up the street with a takeout hot chocolate before realizing it was 10:30 p.m. and she was probably already in bed. Maybe she did me a favor, becoming so unavailable. She'll be too busy for anything once these twins are out in the world, and now I don't have to wonder what if, anymore. What if I wasn't emotionally stunted? What if I was the kind of person who wasn't constantly walking on eggshells, waiting for the other shoe to drop? What if I admitted to myself that Lily Carter was kind of my perfect match in many ways, and she *still* didn't want me?

I tried to keep away at the start. I told her—and I told myself—that she wouldn't need me or want me around, being nauseated and swollen and tired. I assumed she saw us only as the kind of friends who do fun stuff together that pregnant women can't do. But the look on her face when I found out she was hurt... That got me thinking maybe she sees more in me than that.

Now I don't know what to think. All I know is that I was cutting myself off first, before she could do it to me. Fear has a funny way of dictating your actions, I guess. It makes you dance to a tune you can't even hear sometimes.

Hours later, I find myself in the cafeteria, mechanically filling a plate with limp salad and overcooked chicken. Across the room, Lily is sitting with Rose. They're deep in discussion about something that looks pretty serious—twin stuff, no doubt, and she doesn't see me. I'm seeing her tonight, anyway. We're doing dinner, just the two of us and Delilah. My niece loves Lily. We took her to a sleepover at the kids' museum a couple years ago and they somehow wove a whole other world together overnight. Delilah's seen her as a role model ever since.

I said I'd make us all lasagna before we take this "ghosts and gangsters" walk that we've been planning to do for ages, ever since we all watched a documentary on Al Capone. I'm already figuring out a healthy dessert. I'll have to go to Whole Foods for organic strawberries, seeing as we—or rather *she*—can't risk any nasty pesticides right now, and I'm just googling pesticides, as you do, when the spiky-haired assistant nurse who's crushing on me comes up and bats her eyelashes.

"Doctor Montgomery, you need to eat more than that. Someone like you needs to keep their strength up. Outside of the gym, I mean!"

"Someone like me, huh?" I catch Lily looking at me now from across the room. I wait for her to roll her eyes or something but I swear a catch a little pout before she looks sideways. What's that about? I tell the nurse I'm busy and hold up my phone, as if googling pesticides in a cafeteria is normal. I can't think why I'd bother to flirt back, anyway. I don't want to date her. I don't need this nurse to think *anything* about me, really.

Pea's message flashes up. It isn't good and a knot ties itself in my stomach.

Theo, Mom threw out her fan heater today. She said it was whispering secret evil messages! Then she locked Edwina out of the house.

I rub a hand over my face; the harsh lights are too bright. Poor Edwina. Mom's history with intimidating her carers looks set to repeat again, and again. Again with this insanity.

I could go mad replaying the violent storms our dad had to weather before he departed with what was left of his sanity. I swore to myself that I would never be trapped in a relationship like theirs, but Mom's refusing her meds and I'm stuck in the middle all over again.

I slide my phone away before I can type a response I'll regret later. I keep telling Pea we need to force change in some way, send her to rehab where she'll be properly taken care of by a dedicated team, but Pea won't have it.

Usually, I'd escape the hell of it all in my head by distracting myself, by arranging another date, or calling that cute nurse back over, but I can't shake the image of Carter earlier, cradling that newborn. Or how she looked embarrassed in the mirror when I zipped up that dress. I can't get that ultrasound appointment out of my head, either. It didn't feel real before that; or at least, I was able to maintain my distance. The second those tiny dots appeared on the screen it was like a switch flipped for me. I know they're not mine, but it didn't stop all the blood flooding straight into my heart, like the beat I've been drumming to my whole life skipped to the next track and started up again with a whole different rhythm.

I don't even know who I am anymore. I can't trust myself to know what's real. Sometimes, I catch myself looking at Lily and it scares me. I start to imagine a life with her—fatherhood, family, commitment. Things I never thought I'd want, especially after everything Pea and I went through as kids. I had to grow up fast, take on so much more than a kid should. And because of all that, I guess I never let my adult self so much as contemplate becoming someone's rock. It's always been about clinging on to my freedom. But now something's changing in me, and I don't know how to handle it. It's like the ground beneath me is shifting all over again.

It's six thirty. I hurry to put the tomato sauce–covered saucepan and utensils into the dishwasher, clearing the worktop before sprinkling the last of the grated cheese onto the top of my lasagna. I've just closed the oven door on it when the elevator pings in the hallway. Three seconds later, Lily and Delilah are pulling off their jackets in the hallway and Delilah, who has barely stopped to offer me a greeting of any shape or form, is talking ninety miles an hour about the special horse she's been promoted to ride next week, after winning the kids' show-jumping championship.

"Hello to you, too," I say pointedly as she holds her hand up for a high five and then promptly heads to the lounge to claim the entire leather couch and scroll her phone.

"Hope your ears don't hurt too much after all that," I say as Lily follows me into the L-shaped kitchen. "Thanks for offering to pick her up on the way over."

She's wearing the dress I bought her on our shopping trip, and my stomach performs a little acrobatic swoop at the sight of her. It falls just above her knees, a shade of mint green that compliments her eyes. I like her dark brown hair more now that it's growing back out a little, and I like how it's piled on top of her head under a blue bandanna. A few tendrils frame her face, making her look like some sort of casual bohemian goddess from a maternity wear catalog. Why am I staring at her?

"You know I don't mind picking her up, Theo. And you know I think she's great," is all she says, accepting a glass of sparkling water and leaning against the counter, pressing a hand to her bump. She seems a little distracted.

Quickly, I pull one of the stools out from

the breakfast bar and she sits down gratefully, thanking me. I ask if she's okay and she says she's just tired. I say nothing, but when I check on the lasagna, she sighs behind me and starts telling me how Rose was meant to make a vet's appointment for Jasper's FIV vaccine but she forgot, and now Jasper is a week late getting it. I remind her how Jasper is an indoor cat and cannot possibly be at risk of catching a respiratory disease. I also tell her that he himself is a hazard, being a walking, purring furry hairball, and she tells me that for a doctor, I'm surprisingly unfeeling toward living creatures. There's something else going on with her. It's more than the cat.

"Rose is working a lot more lately, huh," I say eventually. I don't miss how her hand keeps moving across her belly in gentle strokes under the counter. From what I've gathered, Rose has been escaping into her work since her divorce, and while she's a devoted sister to Lily, I can see her schedule is making her forget other more important things right now. "Were you in an argument at lunch?"

Lily snaps her eyes up to mine. "Watching me, were you?"

I scoff at her, then busy my hands with the cutlery as I carry it past her to the table. "Don't flatter yourself, Carter."

She sighs. "Fine. We were talking about how she keeps canceling our shopping trip—"

"I took you shopping," I interrupt, gesturing to the dress I bought her. Her cheeks flush and she diverts her eyes, and for some reason I drop a fork to the floor, cursing as I pick it up.

"Yes, and you know I'm very grateful," she says.

"You only let me take you to one store," I remind her, and she tells me she was worried I'd get bored. I get the impression it was more than that. Maybe she felt the change in the air between us, and it freaked her out. She's carrying another man's children, and we're friends.

"Don't get me wrong, Rose means well, and I'm probably being far too needy here…"

"Needy?" I pause to look at her. "How is that being needy? She's your twin sister. You do everything together," I say.

Lily wrinkles her nose. "We used to."

I refill her glass with sparkling water, throw the garlic bread into the oven with the lasagna and she changes the subject to me and my date last night. I pretend it went better than it did, and I don't let on that her hot chocolate went cold in my car before I drove back here and benched five sets before hitting the pillow on my own.

"I'm hungry, Theo," Delilah calls from the couch. I had almost forgotten she was here.

We can see her from the kitchen, but she is too absorbed in her screen to look over her shoulder. It's only when we all sit down at the table and I'm heaping steaming hot, cheesy lasagna onto our plates that she springs back from preteen robot mode into the bubbly kid I adore.

"So have you thought about names yet?" Delilah asks, creating a cheesy tornado from her plate up to her mouth. Lily told Delilah a few weeks ago that she was pregnant, and my niece got surprisingly excited, reading up on twin babies. "What if they're conjoined? I watched a documentary on these conjoined twins in India that had to have their heads separated…"

"They're not conjoined," I say firmly, putting my fork down heavily. Lily is biting back a smile. "Do you even know how rare that is?"

"But if they were, they could be so famous on TikTok," Delilah continues. She waves her fork about enthusiastically as she talks, sending tomato sauce flying across the table. I tell her it's disturbing how much she's thought about this, and try to ignore the sauce splashes on my freshly polished surface. Usually, it would be cleared up in a flash—another echo from childhood, when Mom would fly off the handle over the smallest spill, the tiniest crease in Dad's ironing.

I won't do it while Lily's here.

Thankfully, before we've even cleared our plates, we are all discussing other stuff we've seen on TikTok, and we're laughing, and Lily looks a thousand times happier than when she walked in. As I serve up fresh strawberries with homemade chocolate mousse, she beams from ear to ear.

"Organic?" she says. "I saw the packaging. That's very thoughtful, Theo, thank you."

"I make the odd diversion from my mean-guy routine," I say, deadpan, though the fact that she's noticed makes me feel like I've reached the top of whatever mountain I was just climbing and speared a flag into the highest tree.

"I'm Marcus, and tonight we're going to take a walk on the wild side of Chicago's history—gangsters, ghosts and all!" Marcus, our tour guide, is easily the most excitable person I've met all week, besides Delilah when she talks about horses. She and Lily are listening in rapt concentration, bundled up against the October cold, eating the candy I just bought.

Marcus's tailored suit and the fedora that perches jauntily on his head are obviously supposed to invoke the spirit of Chicago's bygone era of gangsters. The tourists with us are eating it up.

We set off into the streets and I ignore my

phone as it vibrates in my pocket. I already told Pea when we'd have Delilah home, and it would be rude to answer it now. Unless she wants to tell me something else Mom has done.

"Everything okay?" Lily whispers. We've stopped by an unassuming brick wall in a quiet alley that I know already is the site of the Valentine's Day massacre. Marcus explains about the events in 1929, how Al Capone's men gunned down seven members of the North Side Gang and shook Chicago to the core. Delilah is so absorbed. She's wanted to do this tour for ages. I pull a face at Lily.

"Pea is calling me," I tell her.

She shoots me a questioning look and I tell her I'll call when we take a break. Lily doesn't know exactly what's going on with my mother, how we never know which side of her we'll be faced with. How Pea and I suffered as kids. I tend to keep my family stuff to myself after what happened with Tessa. I think I told Lily about Tessa once, the only semiserious girlfriend I've ever had, right before I started at the hospital, before Lily and I met. What I didn't tell her was that Tessa had the misfortune of being at my apartment the day a neighbor unwittingly let Mom into the building. Mom was "self-medicating" on vodka at the time. She yelled at me, yelled at Tessa and broke my kettle by throwing it barely an inch from her head. Tessa broke things off the very next day.

I've always been ashamed, really, that we've never been able to control her. She drove poor Dad to despair and he disowned us *all* because of her. I don't even know where he is, to this day. It's all too crazy and to be honest, too humiliating to try to explain to most people, so Pea and I don't even try. But I can't really ignore my phone anymore as Marcus guides us toward Lincoln Park, to the Biograph Theater.

Pea tells me she endured a half-hour rant from Mom about how the meds she was told to take made her gain weight. Now Pea is too exhausted to drive. She asks if it's all right if Delilah spends the night at my place. I tell her of course. Dee's always had her own room at my place.

When I rejoin the group, they're both absorbed in Marcus's latest story, but Lily has her hands on her lower back. Her knees are slightly bent, like she really needs to sit down. I forget about Mom instantly. I put a hand on her arm and she brushes me off, embarrassed.

"Let's go find you a seat," I say.

"I'm fine, I'll miss the tour. Was that a problem on the phone? Your family?"

I deflect her question. "You've been on your feet all day, Carter. You need to recharge your powers."

"Theo, I said I'm fine. Please don't tell me what to do."

Okay, then. I try not to look pissed while she struggles to pretend she's not getting more uncomfortable by the minute, standing in one spot with no seating in sight. I should've thought about this; she shouldn't be on her feet this long. When we finally move on, Marcus stops at Union Station, and while he's explaining how Capone had secret tunnels running beneath the city, connecting his hideouts, I take a seat by the wall and look at her pointedly. Finally, Lily sits beside me, and I smirk. She smirks back.

"You don't always have to look out for me, you know." She sniffs.

"Who else is going to, Carter?" I say before I can think. She's so stubborn.

I regret it instantly when I see the look on her face. "You think I'm stupid, doing this alone, don't you?" Her words come out a little choked and her green eyes search mine, almost daring me to lie.

"I think you're brave," I tell her carefully as Delilah sits next to me, shoving the empty candy box at me so I can dispose of it.

"Nice try."

"You're not alone, anyway. Don't expect the violins just yet," I tell her, tossing the candy box into the trash and nudging her. Instead of shoving me away, she rests her soft head on my shoulder, then buries her face in my coat. "Carter, just ask for help when you need it. Don't be stubborn."

We sit there as the cold drizzle plays in the air, and I rest my head gently on hers. I want her to ask me for help. I want to be involved. I want to buy organic strawberries and rub her feet and I don't know what any of this means. I need to get away.

The medical conference in Florida next week cannot come soon enough.

CHAPTER SIX

THE ALARM BLARES from the far incubator and sends a jolt of fear straight through me. Baby Mia Malone. I can barely see her through the plastic walls of the incubator as I pull on my gloves and maternity gown and call for Amber, all in a matter of milliseconds, but I know something is very wrong. Born at just twenty-seven weeks, she weighs barely over two pounds. My heart aches every time I look at her.

Her oxygen saturation levels are dropping—fast. I watch the numbers flash on the monitor: eighty-two, seventy-eight. Seventy-four... My breath catches in my throat as Amber appears. We can't afford to lose a second.

"We need to intubate now," I say, my voice miraculously steadier than I feel. I grab the laryngoscope, my hands moving on autopilot, and I carefully open Mia's tiny mouth. Her skin is so delicate and pale it seems like it could tear at the slightest touch. Her breaths are shallow; her chest is barely rising. I try to focus, try to block out the fears that threaten to overwhelm me now every time I encounter an emergency with someone's child. I've done this so many times before, but never with two fragile babies inside me, and I'd be lying if I didn't project every outcome onto them. It's selfish, but it's unstoppable. Rose says I need to get used to it, and she means it in the nicest possible way.

I guide the tube into her airway. Amber is quick to connect the ventilator, and I hold my breath, praying for that first *whoosh* of air.

For a terrifying moment, nothing happens. My heart pounds in my ears, and the room seems to blur around me. Mia's tiny life is in my hands. This can't be it. It cannot end like this.

And then, we hear it—the soft, steady *whoosh* of the ventilator. I glance up at the monitor and watch in relief as the numbers start to climb: seventy-eight, eighty-three, eighty-eight…

"Oh, thank goodness." I let out a breath, gently stroking Mia's tiny hand with my gloved finger. Her chest is moving more rhythmically now, but I know we're not out of the woods yet. Mia's lungs are so fragile, they could collapse at any moment, or her tiny heart could give out from the strain. I turn to Amber, my voice urgent. "Get me the surfactant. We need to stabilize her lungs."

Amber prepares the medication while I keep

my eyes glued to the vitals. Babies like Mia don't have the surfactant their lungs need to stay open, and without it, the ventilator will only be a temporary fix. I can't afford to think the worst. I administer the surfactant through the tube, watching the baby's squishy face for any signs of distress. Her tiny body tenses, and I feel my own muscles clench in response. I will her to hang in there a little longer, but seconds feel like hours as I wait.

Slowly, so slowly, her oxygen levels begin to rise again. Ninety-two, ninety-five, ninety-eight… The alarms are silenced, replaced by the soothing rhythm of the ventilator. I know I'm getting far too emotional because of my condition, but I feel the tears prick at the corners of my eyes as Amber squeezes my shoulder, tells me we did it, that Mia will be all right. I know what she's thinking, though. Everyone here thinks I'm a walking liability, probably. I miss Theo. Thank goodness I'm seeing him tonight. He's finally back from his trip.

The thought makes my skin prickle in excitement, but I snuff it out fast. I've been having this thought about missing him since he left and I don't like it. I shouldn't miss Theo when he's not here, but then, it's not just at work that I've come to rely on him being around, popping up on his breaks, taking me down to the cafeteria. And I haven't really heard from him much since he left.

"Will you be all right from here?" Amber asks carefully.

"Of course," I assure her, though the question echoes in my head. Will I? The what-ifs surrounding my own pregnancy keep mounting up, selfishly. What if something like this happens to me? What if something happens to my babies when Rose isn't here? When Dad isn't here? Or next time Theo is away?

"Hey, look at you!" Rose looks up as I dump my bag on the kitchen table. "Finally wearing clothes that fit?" she teases, eyeing my new outfit.

I changed into the new pants and cozy oversize sweater before driving home. I never leave work in my scrubs if I can help it. I enjoy some separation between my work life and home life, unlike my twin sister.

"I'm sorry it took us so long to go shopping, but it's nice that Theo took you to that one store and bought you that dress to tide you over."

"I know," I say, smiling at the memory, before a shiver of something like fear snakes along my spine and startles me. There was a moment in the changing room, when he zipped me up, when I swear my body did something strange in his presence. A feeling of longing that I totally was not expecting almost took me out. Just feeling the brush of his fingers on my skin, and his admiring eyes on me. I was so embarrassed I insisted we only go to that one store.

"I'm a hormonal mess," I say by way of an excuse, even though I didn't tell Rose how I felt. "And I still feel like I'm turning into a whale."

"Please," Rose says, rolling her eyes. I sit down at the bench and Jasper winds his way around my legs, purring. Her expression softens. "Lil, you look amazing. Makes me a little jealous, you know?"

"Jealous?" I frown at her, stirring the non-caffeinated herbal tea she puts before me. "You could still have this, too, if you wanted." I tell her she's young and beautiful and that it's not like her biological clock has hit snooze all of a sudden.

"Sure," she sighs, tracing the rim of her own cup. I know she's thinking about David and what he did. The affair stole her confidence more than her physical ability to chase her dreams. We were always the "flower girls" growing up, the "prettiest in class" according to, well…most of the guys who wanted to date one or both of us.

She sits up straighter. "A thirty-four-year-old divorcée who works around the clock. Can't you see them all lining up to date me?"

"Stop it," I say, and she knows I mean it. "You don't need a man to have a baby, anyway—look at where you work."

"It's a family I want, Lils," she sighs, and I shut my mouth. We don't talk about Dr. David Andersson anymore; we just despise him in secret. "You need to stop working so hard, make room for… I don't know, a life."

"A life, huh? What is that exactly?" She raises an eyebrow just as her pager beeps insistently. "No time for a life, apparently. Duty calls." She stands abruptly, the chair screeching against the floor as she leans down to peck my cheek. "Evening team meet, then dinner. You'll be okay?"

"See you later," I call after her, and it's only when her coat is a blur in the doorway that I remember I won't, because I'm meeting Theo soon.

My heart does that weird fluttery thing in my throat again when I think about walking into McFadden's and seeing him in our usual spot, but I snuff it out again. I don't know what's been going on lately. No, I do… It's my hormones. My stupid hormones. Maybe my babies want a daddy, seeing as their own is not in the picture. Which is my fault as much as his. I don't need Anthony. He was a sperm donor of sorts. I'm fine with that.

I sip my tea, trying to dislodge the idea of me

and Theo. I guess it makes sense that I'm over-thinking it all. Hormones are one thing but also, Theo Montgomery is the only male in my life besides Dad who pays me that much attention now that I'm pregnant! I put him in the friend zone when we met for a reason, though. He's a verified playboy with more commitment issues than designer shirts, and that's saying something. And I'm not even out for a partner; I'm a terrible partner. Plus, look at Rose. David may well have been one of the country's most sought-after cardiothoracic surgeons, but his own after-hours meetings were less about performing lung surgeries and more about performing God knows what on his surgical technologist. He shattered Rose. They were trying for a baby at the time.

Rose and I might slip from time to time, wanting more, wanting men. But we know we can't count on them. That's why we bought the house. *Our* house. Our nonconventional family house, just the flower girls and Jasper, forever.

Well...until you guys come along, I think, stroking a hand over my belly in the mirror.

My silhouette is changing by the week now. Will Theo think I'm a whale, too? Why do I care so much?

Sometime later, the familiar boozy-bleach smell of McFadden's surrounds me. I untangle my scarf and remove my coat and search the crowd for that familiar tousle of dark hair.

"Over here!" Theo calls me over from a different table to the one we usually have, with its high stools. He's scored the sofa seat with the plush velvet cushions. Above us, a forgotten paper Halloween pumpkin has escaped the post-Halloween cleanup. How is it November already?

"Who did you have to fight to get this seat on game night?" I ask him, sliding my bump in beside him. He moves the table out slightly to make sure I can fit. A TV blares the NFL game on the wall and he jokes over the din about fighting a grandma and sending her back out onto the street before he stands to get me a drink. He's wearing a white Henley, tight on the chest and arms, tapering sharply down the waist to his jeans. He looks hot, but then, when doesn't he, and when doesn't he *know* he looks hot?

I lean back against his coat, which he's draped on the back of the couch. It smells of him, and as he turns back toward me carrying my drink, my whole stomach joins in with my heart for one big flutter. No, wait. It's more than just Theo causing this. My hands fly to my bulge. "Oh, my…"

"What?" Theo's figure casts a shadow over me. I look up at his concerned face before I grin.

"I felt them. I felt them move." It feels so strange.

He looks alarmed for a second and just kind of hovers, looking at me like I'm an alien. His face makes me laugh.

"Got you a ginger ale," he says, sliding a frosty glass toward me. "Hope the gas doesn't get them even more excited in there."

"It's happening again," I tell him in awe, still laughing. This is the first time I've felt them. I'm almost twenty-one weeks now so it's normal, but still, it's unlike anything I've ever experienced. So strange and unsettling, yet kind of comforting at the same time. Like they're fluffing their little nest, making more room to grow. I keep my hands pressed to my belly over my new smart pants while Theo looks sideways, then at me, then at his drink and then up at the game.

"Wanna feel, Doctor?" I ask him. I fully expect him to shake his head and refuse. He's not my doctor, he's my friend, and for a second I feel silly for even offering—this clearly weirds him out. But I think his curiosity wins. Slowly, he reaches a tentative hand to my midsection and I press my hand over his, guiding it. Sure enough, another kick comes from within and Theo's eyes grow wide, before lighting up like they did in the clinic that day.

"They're going to be better boxers than me,"

he says, pressing his warm, big hand flatter to my belly. His palm against my flesh feels far more intimate than I expected, just like it did in the store changing room. His careful touch sends a flush to my cheeks before I bury it in my hair, but I'm caught like a rabbit in the deep blue hues of his eyes when he grins at me. I'm cast back to that night at his place over dinner, with Delilah. He went out of his way to prepare all that for me. And then on the tour, he was so careful to look after me… It all spins around in my head as I look at him now.

Good Lord, my hormones are putting me through it right now.

"You can teach them self-defense," I say, distracted. "I mean, if you want to be in their lives once they're born."

He looks genuinely confused and my heart soars when he asks, "Why wouldn't I?" Then he adds, "Not that they'll need my help, knowing how kick-ass you are, Carter."

The barman, Freddy D, interrupts us. We know him, of course. He tells me I'm looking great, asks if we want food and we say no, and as they talk I can't help wondering why I thought Theo wouldn't want to be involved. Grayson got to me again, like he always does when I'm enjoying being myself. I second-guessed everything I did and said around him. What would

Theo think of me if he knew how long I put up with that?

Suddenly, I realize what Freddy D is telling Theo.

"That chick you abandoned here on your bad date the other week? I wanted to thank you, man. She went home with a friend of mine. They've been inseparable ever since, if you know what I mean."

Theo clears his throat. I glare at Freddy D for obvious reasons, but then his words sink in. Theo abandoned a date early? Why? Especially if the woman would have gone home with him, as Freddy so licentiously implied. Doesn't sound like him at all.

His phone buzzes on the table. It's Pea. He cuts it off. I ask him why.

"It's nothing important," he says quickly in a way that implies something important is definitely going on, something I've missed. I tell him so and my adrenaline spikes harder than it just did over hearing that Theo left a date early. Why does he keep brushing me off when I ask about his family?

"Theo, if something's going on—" I continue, but he cuts me off.

"Tell me, Carter, have you heard from what's-his-name again? The babies' father?"

Instantly, I'm on the offense. I turn away from

him, nurse my drink. "I'm sending him updates. It's only polite. Sometimes he replies. Sometimes he doesn't."

"Is that disappointing for you?" He's trying to sound casual, casting an eye to the game again, which I have zero interest in right now. This mix of emotions swirling inside me is so confusing. Plus, I'm annoyed that he's clearly keeping things from me. And that I am giving Anthony updates on the twins despite the fact that he barely replies, for the simple, messed-up reason that I don't want him to think badly of me for absolutely *anything* at all.

"I don't know, Theo. He asked for updates, so as not to sound like a completely disinterested party, I suppose."

"If you *know* he doesn't care, why are you giving him updates?" He leans in, all trace of distraction gone, his blue eyes focusing intently on me. I swallow. Theo can goof around with the best of them but likewise he can be *so* intense.

"Because he's the father."

"Father of the year, Carter. Top points to him for communicating solely by text message whenever he feels like it, when you're over here a million miles away with…"

"With no one? Is that what you were thinking?"

He scowls, and the dent between his eyebrows

deepens. "What about what *you* need? Won't this mess with your head down the line?"

"You think I should just cut him off?" I stare at him. Yes, I'm mad at him, but I want his opinion now, because honestly, hearing him this passionate is kind of hot. I wasn't aware he cared this much about my relationships, or nonrelationships as the case may be. I've never said anything to him about why it ended with Grayson before we met, and he's never really probed.

"I don't want to see you get hurt," he says simply, drumming his fingers on the table, the game forgotten.

"And I don't want my babies getting hurt, either. I'm just trying to do the right—"

I'm cut off by a deafening cheer as something in the game sends the bar into an uproar. Before I've even finished my sentence, or had time to move, someone, a man, is careening backward into our table and the whole thing slides toward us by several inches, right up hard against my stomach. It knocks the wind out of me for a moment. I can hardly think, let alone register what just happened, but in the space of three seconds I'm covered in sticky drinks, Theo is shoving the table away into the crowd of men who fell onto it, and somehow I'm on the floor, telling my babies and myself to breathe.

CHAPTER SEVEN

MY HEART THROTTLES straight to a sprint when Lily's hands go to her stomach. Suddenly, I'm on my knees in front of her. The clamor of the bar fades to a dull roar in my ears. My hands are already on autopilot, gently probing around the area that took the hit.

"Talk to me, Lil. Do we need help here?"

"We're okay." She's sucking in deep lungfuls of air, biting her lip. Her green eyes meet mine with her customary bravado, but I see the pain shimmering from their depths and it makes my chest tighten. "It hurts a little…right here," she says. Her hands shake as she holds them just below her rib cage.

"Take slow breaths for me, all right? In and out. You're doing great," I tell her. I'm trying to keep my voice steady for her sake as I run through the checklist in my head: assess, stabilize, manage pain, but there is only one of the three I can do right here. I need to get her out.

A crowd has gathered around us, and I order

them to move, then urge Lily's eyes to mine. "We're going to get you out of here. Keep breathing."

She winces and her breath hitches, but she follows my lead, her chest rising and falling more evenly after a few tries. My gaze flicks over her face, taking in every detail. Pale, she's gone pale. "Any dizziness or blurred vision?" I ask, keeping one hand on her shoulder, while someone drapes her coat over her in concern.

"No, nothing like that," she manages, gripping my arm. "Theo, we need to…"

"I'm going to help you up, okay? Can you manage?"

She takes my arm and with some effort, we get her to her feet. I move the table back even farther, and the crowd around us shuffles to make room. But just as she's stable, she wobbles, and I loop an arm around her waist to support her. On second thought, I'm not going to risk a fall at this point. Quickly, I pick her up in my arms and head for the door. Her weight is nothing compared to the heavy dread settling in my chest.

"Hold on to me," I say, more for my own reassurance than hers. "We're going to get you checked out ASAP."

"Theo…" Her voice wavers close to my ear. Her arms around my shoulders tighten. The adrenaline feels like liquid fire in my veins, and the urge to guard her with my life intensifies a thousandfold, but this is not the time to try to decipher what this weird new arrangement of emotions is every time I'm in Lily's presence lately.

"Evergreen's closest. I'm driving you." My words are a command, not a suggestion. I put her down carefully in the underground parking lot and unlock the car. She agrees, even though I know she doesn't want to mix business with her pregnancy. The other place, Dawson's, is too far away from here with the traffic. Besides, I work at Evergreen. I run the ER and this is an emergency.

Carefully, I help her into the back seat, tell her to keep on breathing, as if she doesn't know the drill already. This also means she knows that things can go wrong. Very wrong. "This is just standard procedure, you know that."

"Of course. I tell all my patients to arrive by sports car," she says through a grimace, and I tell her not to make jokes, to be quiet, to breathe.

She clasps at my hand, just as I'm about to shut the door. "I'm serious, I trust you," she says, and the look in her eyes…it's like she's lit a rocket under me. I don't break the speed limit on the way to the hospital, but I don't think I've ever reached it so quickly. The drive is a blur. My mind is already racing through protocols and potential complications. The silence between us is filled with the soft sounds of Lily's measured breaths and I can't risk saying anything else, but I know this is my fault for taking her to McFadden's. I wanted her to think we can still be normal. *I* wanted to think we could still be normal. We both know what just happened wasn't good.

"She needs attention, ASAP. Let's get her to bay two!"

I'm met on the forecourt. I've already called ahead, and two of my team members are waiting with a wheelchair. I help Lily into it and rush to park the car so I can get inside. It takes me all of four minutes.

I find her in bay two and I pull on my scrubs in record time.

"Doctor Montgomery, you're not on shift," a nurse tells me, trying to wave me away.

Lily's voice stops her. "It's all right. I want him here."

Several team members look between us in confusion.

"Sorry if I'm a drama queen," Lily says next, and I frown in her direction. "I'm not used to being on this side of things."

"Stop apologizing. Why do you always do that? Focus on yourself," I tell her, and she presses her hands to her belly, wincing. For someone so set in her ways about certain things, she can be surprisingly self-sabotaging sometimes. "Did they move again?" I ask her.

"I think so."

"That's a good sign," I remind her, and she presses her lips together. We both know the alternative is just not a viable option.

"Doctor Montgomery," one of the techs acknowledges me. "What do we need?"

"We need an urgent ultrasound. Please page radiology right away. Also, page the on-call OB-GYN specialist to come down to the ER immediately."

Lily's on the gurney in seconds, her face all pinched in discomfort. I watch with my heart in my throat as the sonographer appears and preps the equipment, and Lily helps smear the cold gel around her own stomach. I fetch a bunch of paper towels and rub it from her hands for her; she shouldn't have done that, but I know she's probably not thinking clearly. I hear her take a sharp intake of breath as the cold tool is placed upon her, and without thinking I take her sticky hand.

The hum of the machine fills the space as images flicker to life on the screen. Two tiny hearts beating. Relief washes over me but it's premature, I know—I have to wait for the final word.

"Vitals are stable, Doctor Montgomery," a nurse reports.

"Keep monitoring her," I instruct, never taking my eyes off the screen. I want this to be over for her. People are looking. Let them look.

I've flirted and hit on her before, but I've always been happy with Carter as my friend, really. Nothing else would work, anyway, not least because of Mom. Tessa proved that. I'll never forget her face when she was forced to duck that flying kettle. Every time we hear of something else she's done to send a carer packing, I'm thrown right back to the boxing ring we called a living room—me in the corner, Pea's face pressed into my chest while I inch us closer and closer to the door so we could finally make a run from whatever Mom was using as missiles to launch at Dad that day besides words. But every time I back off from Lily lately, something draws me back even stronger. I spent the whole time at that conference in Florida wondering where the baby daddy was, thinking how I should go out, meet some women, get this weird new set of emotions out of my system, and then doing nothing about it.

"Looks like they're determined. They're not hurt at all," the sonographer finally announces. I blink as her words settle into reality. Lily lets out half of a strangled sob before covering her mouth.

"Thank God," she breathes out, and my heart thuds as she exhales deeply with her eyes closed. The connection is something beyond friendship now; for me, anyway. I can't make complete sense of it. It's visceral, a tether that feels like it tightens with every moment we share, including this one. Before I know it, everyone's left the room except me.

"You're gonna be okay, Carter," I say, resisting the urge to sweep a few matted strands of damp hair from her face. I know I should excuse myself now, leave as more doctor than friend, but her eyes root me to the bedside and I can't help imagining, under different circumstances, if things *were* different, I'd probably kiss her forehead or something right now. Why the hell do I want to kiss Lily's forehead? As if that wouldn't just make me want to kiss her mouth.

"Theo," she says, and her eyes are full of the kind of questions I don't know how to answer. What if something else like this happens? What if next time it does, there's no doctor present? Doing this alone is not a good idea, not as good as Lily thinks it is, but it's not my place to always be there, just in case. I'm her friend. Nothing more.

Her phone buzzes, and I catch the name on the screen. Anthony. Him, the father.

I bite my lip. I mean, I guess it's her prerogative if she wants to involve him. And her kids will one day want to know who he is, probably, but it's causing her additional stress. Stress that I shouldn't add to by questioning her about it.

"What you said before, about involving him. I'm sorry things got so…heated," I say.

She looks away. "Maybe you're right. Maybe I shouldn't be involving him."

"Look, don't listen to me," I tell her. "I don't know anything about what you're going through."

"The same as I don't know anything about what *you're* going through, Theo," she says pointedly.

"Me?" My shoulders tense. She sighs in frustration.

"All the calls? All the messages. Is your family in the secret service or something? I don't want to impose but it's hard to be around you sometimes, knowing you're keeping things from me. At least I'm telling you about Anthony, even if it makes me an idiot."

"You're not an idiot. Stop all this self-deprecating talk. What is that about, anyway? It's not just your hormones, Lily."

She tuts at me loudly. "Stop changing the subject."

I search for the right words to say. I hate that my secrecy is upsetting to her; I hate that more than anything. I've learned to protect myself by keeping people at arm's length, avoiding emotional vulnerability to prevent the pain of abandonment I felt as a kid. It's textbook psychology, a blatant manifestation of my fractured emotional intelligence, which Lily has noticed and interpreted as righteous entitlement. I'm allowed to know her, but she can't know me. She's right; it's not fair.

I open my mouth to speak but I don't actually know what to say. At least, I can't put it into words; it's complicated. Telling her anything means telling her everything. I study the poster for the upcoming annual fundraiser on the back of the door. We both went last year. We drank champagne and dared each other to do terrible moves on the dance floor. I think I won. Those were good times. Way less complicated.

"Theo?"

I hold my hands up. "I guess there's some stuff I never talk about when it comes to my family."

"What kind of stuff?"

"It's my mother—" I start, racking my brain as to how to explain. I'm interrupted, however, by the door. It bangs open with such force it reverberates against the walls and Rose barges in, her eyes storms of fury. "Theo, what the hell?"

"Rose," I start, moving to intercept her, but she's a cyclone of indignation, stepping around me, straight to Lily's side. "Are you okay?"

"I'm fine," she assures her, adjusting her pillows again before I take over.

"We were at McFadden's," I explain. "You know how it gets on game night...some guys got a little too excited—"

"It happened *so* fast," Lily repeats, almost on top of me, but Rose is only looking at me now.

"McFadden's? Theo! You took my pregnant sister to a bar full of drunks?" Her voice scales up and I rub my jaw, feeling Lily tense beside me. Her fingers brush mine briefly. Rose's eyes catch the movement and she purses her lips together, seemingly composing herself. "You scared me," she says to Lily. "Both of you." She glares at me again.

"It wasn't Theo's fault," Lily tells her. "He knew I wanted to do all the things we used to do..."

"But you can't, Lily."

Lily closes her eyes, and I know she's holding herself back from snapping. "I'm just grateful he was there. He drove me straight here."

Rose just glowers and Lily lowers her voice. She's doing her best not to make a scene. "What was I meant to do, Rose, stay home alone again? I'm pregnant. I'm not disabled."

I step back as they glare at each other, forces of nature, alike in so many ways you'd almost think they were identical. Eventually, Rose huffs some kind of apology. She reaches down to stroke a hand along her sister's cheek. "I'm just so relieved you're all right."

"Thanks to Theo."

I watch as Rose's features soften, the rigid lines of her mouth relaxing. She takes a deep breath, then turns toward me as I straighten some equipment needlessly at the other end of the room. Her eyes are still glinting with the remnants of worry and something a little like gratitude, maybe. It's hard to tell. It could be loathing. "Thank you for being there," she says, finally, slowly. "I should've been more available."

"Rose…" Lily reaches out, grabbing her sister's hand. "You're here now. That's what counts."

Rose tells her she will put her and the babies first from now on, and I excuse myself, giving them space. The weight of the day and everything we've now left unsaid feels like a bowling ball pressing heavy on my chest. Seeing Lily loved and cared for eases some of the tension knotting my insides, but the knots are also a reminder of why I've kept these kinds of feelings at bay since that whole thing with Tessa. Mom is a liability; I'm not in a stable place; I'm not what anyone needs, not as far as anything re-sembling partnership is concerned. I have to let Rose step up and remember my proper place as Lily's colleague and friend.

CHAPTER EIGHT

WHAT A MORNING. Not only have I been experiencing severe back ache since 7:00 a.m., but I've also just attended an emergency C-section down in ER and the sight of blood, for the first time in years, made me feel quite queasy. Heading for the elevator, I'm picturing the bubble bath I'll be pouring myself when I get home when Theo's voice calls me back.

"Carter, glad I caught you. Do you have a moment?"

The air between us crackles with a new energy the second I meet his eyes. I get that familiar flash of warmth, the one that just bubbles up now whenever he is near. Something changed that day at McFadden's, maybe even before our heated words about Anthony. Neither of us has brought it up, and I can tell he still doesn't want to talk about whatever he has going on, either. I wonder if that's why he's been extra "busy" lately. Or maybe he's been busy with his secret life, whatever it is that's going on with his mom that he never finished telling me about. I've been wanting to ask, but he's made sure that we've hardly seen each other.

Anyway, now is not the time to analyze his actions, or my own wild heartbeat around him.

"We thought it was appendicitis," he tells me, ushering me back into the chaotic ER, toward a closed curtain. "But the ultrasound showed us otherwise." He keeps his voice low as he continues, handing me the chart. "She's seventeen, Carter. She doesn't know she's pregnant."

A scream takes all the words from my mouth as he sweeps the curtain aside. A teenage girl with matted brown hair and a clammy forehead is clutching her abdomen, crying out in pain on the bed. I'm just stepping around to speak to her when Theo takes my arm. The shock in his eyes throws me. "She's crowning."

My heart thumps erratically, adrenaline flushing through me as I process the words. The teenage girl on the stretcher before us has been completely oblivious to the life growing inside her until this very moment.

"Wh-what's going on?" she stammers, her eyes wide with shock as people flurry around her and I take her hand.

"Sweetheart, you're going to have a baby," I say gently, locking eyes with her. "Right now."

"Baby? But I—I didn't know… I can't be…"

Panic weaves through her voice, crescendoing into an almost hysterical pitch as the pain takes hold again.

"Easy, we've got you," Theo reassures her.

"Where is the OB-GYN? We need them here, stat!" I call out.

"Called for, but we don't have time," Theo replies tersely, glancing at me. "We have to do this, Doctor Carter."

"Of course," I acknowledge, my hands already moving to gather what we need. "Okay, you're going to feel a lot of pressure, but you need to push when I tell you to," I instruct the girl. "Can you do that for us?" I squeeze her hand for emphasis and she nods, tears spilling down her cheeks. I can't help but admire her bravery. This poor girl is so scared and unprepared, yet here she is, about to become a mother in the most unexpected way possible. Imagine!

"Ready?" Theo glances at me again. I support her legs, encouraging her through each contraction, while Theo remains focused, guiding the baby.

"Almost there," I cheer her on, while sweat beads along my brow in sympathy. My back still hurts like hell, but this is not about me. "You're doing amazing."

"Next push, come on," Theo urges, and with one more monumental effort, the cries of a newborn pierce the air and it feels like I can finally breathe, too.

Theo passes the newborn to me, his eyes locking on to mine again. "Doctor Carter, NICU, now."

"Is—is the baby okay?" the girl asks as I take the baby from his hands.

"We're going to make sure he's just fine," I hear him say as I head for the elevator.

My head is whirling. That poor young woman must be in a state of complete shock. What will she do now?

Hours later, after the chaos has settled and the baby is safe under my colleagues' supervision, I find myself walking alongside Theo through the empty parking lot. He's talking about the young mother, asking if she's getting help, and I tell him everything I know. I can't help how the whole thing made me feel even more grateful that I have so much support around me, even though I'm going through this without a man. I also can't help the way my mind goes to Theo now, whenever I do picture a man at my side, despite the fact he's been distant again lately. It's crossed my mind that maybe he feels a little guilty that the last time we hung out I got hurt.

He's changed out of his scrubs and ironed coat into jeans that hug his thighs just right, and a simple black T-shirt under his thick winter coat. The words *effortlessly handsome* spring to mind. He's perfected the kind of casual that makes my heart do a traitorous little flutter. I should not be letting my raging hormones get the better of me. I have enough to deal with right now without reading into Theo's push and pull approach to our friendship at every given turn. Besides, Rose wants to take me to a pregnancy yoga class tonight, and ever since she's decided to put our sisterhood first—as much as her schedule will allow, of course—I've been enjoying our twin time.

He asks me what I'm doing tonight, and the question breaks the silence as he digs for the keys to his car.

"Yoga for whales," I tell him, trying to focus on anything but the way his shirt stretches across his chest as he moves. It's a futile attempt; my mind betrays me, flashing back to the warrior Highlander–like protection of his arms around me as he carried me out of McFadden's the other week. I remember his familiar scent, clean like his apartment, how I breathed it in for comfort. He was comfort. I needed him and he was there. He was more than there; he was my hero.

"Is that right," he says, stopping by his car, giving me that look. "Both the flower girls, together?"

"Yep, it was Rose's idea."

He waits for me to talk, because he knows as well as I do that Rose was less than impressed at me going out to bars, and anywhere, in fact, where trouble might befall me. It wasn't him she was mad at specifically. I know that, and I'd hope that he does, too. She was mad at herself for not making more time for me, to look after me, like we promised each other we always would.

I don't tell him how it's starting to feel like it did before I met Grayson, because he doesn't know about what I put myself through with that man—he'd think me an idiot if he did. Instead, I tell him how it feels like it did before *she* met David, before David started stealing her away from me at every chance. It's tough when the closest person to you in the whole entire world meets someone else who's simultaneously trying to be the closest person to them in the whole entire world. Her ex didn't understand the twin thing, but then, not many people do. We are cosmically bound to each other. Each little fracture, like a minor falling out, or a boyfriend who demands all your time, needs healing for the world to be right again.

When I stop talking, I realize Theo's head is slightly cocked and he's looking at me with such interest, it feels like I've just been beamed down for inspection from a spaceship. "Well, I'm happy you two are getting your vibe back."

"What are *you* doing tonight?" I ask. When he smiles like this, with his lips still tight and a twinkle in his eyes, I get that same warm flush throughout my whole body, and this time it doesn't stop at my skin. It goes between my legs and makes me shuffle awkwardly on the spot. Curse these raging hormones.

"Going home. Eventually," he answers. I can see a glint of something unreadable in his blue gaze now.

"I get it, Theo," I say stiffly. He's clearly going on a date right now, and it bothers me more than it should. "Well, have fun on your date. I guess I'll see you tomorrow."

I start to head toward my own car.

"How do you know I'm going on a date, Carter?" he calls, and I pause with my back to him a moment before turning around.

"Because you don't look as shabby as you usually do," I say. "Did Delilah dress you again?"

"Not this time."

The light from the lamppost casts a halo around him, and he stands there smirking at me infuriatingly in his designer navy wool coat, still unzipped, despite his breath casting little clouds every time he speaks. Why does he have to look at me like this? Maybe he always has, but now the emotions are tangling up with each other inside me—intrigue, excitement and something else, something I don't think I'll ever dare go for again, not after Grayson. It feels a lot like desire.

He takes a few more steps toward me, away from his own car. "From your admirable attempt at wit, Carter, am I right to think you're jealous?"

"Please," I scoff, rolling my eyes, even though something in my chest tightens at the thought.

He leans casually against my car as I search for my keys. I am quite jealous. This is wild. And I do have to talk about what's going on, because if I don't I'll go crazy, and I'm sick of holding things back.

"Listen. Ever since that night at McFadden's—" I start, then I hesitate. Do I really want to go there with him looking like every woman's dream and me feeling like a tired, hormonal mess? But something compels me to continue. "You've been distant again, Theo. Don't tell me I'm imagining it."

"I thought it was best for me to give you and Rose space to work things out. And look, it's working," he explains calmly. He locks his eyes on to mine with an intensity that makes my heart stutter. I wonder if he's really just been going on another endless stream of dates without his pregnant friend killing his mojo, which, to be fair, he has every right to do. He can do what he wants.

"It's been working," I confirm. Whatever's going on, I'm glad he understands that there was something to work out with me and Rose in the first place. The twin thing is a mystery to a lot of people; it always was to Grayson. "You told me something was going on with your mom," I say now, crossing my arms. "Is that still the case?"

He scratches at his chin and finally zips up his coat. He does it a little too hard. "It never ends, Carter," he says.

"What never ends? What is it?"

"She's pretty sick," he replies, and I swallow, pressing a hand to my bump.

"I'm so sorry. Why didn't you say anything?"

He tenses. "Because, what we have, Carter, is an escape from all that, and I don't particularly enjoy talking about it."

I'm jarred for a second by the fact that he's never seen what we have as anything more than an escape, but then…he's been an escape for me, too. I was always too ashamed to tell him much about Grayson. We've both been keeping things from each other.

"Theo, how sick is she?"

He pulls a face, tells me it's nothing anyone can control, and I fire a couple more questions at him, which he deflects expertly until I'm annoyed again. Rose would have a field day with this, I think. She's been poking and prodding about Theo ever since I told her he carried me out of the bar and personally drove me to the hospital. I wasn't exactly thrilled to find myself at Evergreen that night. I guess I feared the whispers and pitying glances and the fact that I was taking up space. But they've been nothing but supportive ever since, whereas Theo's done that disappearing act thing again, physically and emotionally. My getting hurt is one possible reason for the distance, but maybe he's picked up on my new feelings toward him—the last thing the eternally single bachelor probably wants to deal with. Pressing him like this puts me on edge as much as it apparently does him. Our proximity feels charged now, like the air before a storm. His posture has changed; he's guarded.

"Okay, well, don't let me keep you," I say.

I finally unlock the car and lower my weary body into the seat, careful to fit my bulge behind the steering wheel. Theo watches through the window. Then he taps on the glass and I roll it down.

"The fundraiser thing over the weekend. Black tie, silent auction, the whole deal. You've seen the posters."

"Same as last year, different venue," I remark, turning the key in the ignition.

"We're going again, right?" he says.

I frown at him. "You want me to go with you? Why? Did your date cancel?"

"I didn't ask anyone else," he admits, rubbing the back of his neck.

"So, you want *me* to be your date?"

"I want you to be my better philanthropic half. My wingwoman," Theo clarifies quickly.

"Your wingwoman? Really, looking like this?" I'm kind of laughing now but the word tastes strangely bitter on my tongue. I've been his wingwoman many, many times before and it's never bothered me till now, now that he's retreating, forcing out my clingy side, damn him. On top of my hormones, this is doubly bad.

"Think about it?" he asks. "It'll be fun. I said I'd help with the banner. Some of Delilah's horsey friends are helping to paint it. I'm also putting the gift baskets together."

"Look at you, getting all involved," I tease, although how sweet is it of him to volunteer?

"I'm more about getting the gossip like we did last year. And the free dinner." He winks at me and I smile. It does sound fun, actually. I haven't been out to anything like this in ages.

"I'll think about it," I reply. Why is my pulse racing?

"Great," Theo says. "I know you love helping out for a good cause."

"I'll wear my maternity superhero cape," I add, and suddenly I'm presented with a flashback to a friend's art exhibition that Grayson took me to, several months before I ended things for good. I wasn't allowed to speak to anyone there except him, and he took me aside at regular intervals to either praise me for how well I was doing, or berate me for making too much eye contact with people. It was after that, when I came home visibly shaken, that Rose confronted me, and we hatched the plan for me to move my stuff out of his place and into the rental she had at the time.

Theo glances at his watch. "I should probably get going."

"Hot date can't wait, right?"

He nods, lifting his weight from my car. "Inexcusable acts of tardiness don't go down well with my sister, Carter. She's not the forgiving kind. Neither is Delilah."

I open my mouth to respond, then close it as my cheeks start to flush. Okay. So he's meeting Peonie and his niece tonight. And now I feel like a total idiot. I almost put my serious face on and demand he tell me what's really going on with his family, but he's just reminded me I'm the "fun friend" to go out and get the gossip with, the one to eat free dinners with, the one who teases him about who he might be dating, and suddenly I'm biting my tongue, pressing a hand to my bulge. That's how he sees me. The fun friend, who's expecting another man's babies. I won't embarrass myself by slipping into some unwelcome counselor or partner role; he clearly doesn't want that from me. And I can't seem to stay mad at him.

"Have fun, tell them I say hi," I say as I slip into gear. I am utterly exhausted. At least I have a "bit of fun" lined up with him, even if it's the platonic kind, as usual.

CHAPTER NINE

THE CLANK OF metal on metal reverberates through the penthouse as I heave the dumbbells above my head. It's one way of shedding the weight of the morning shift just now at the hospital. We managed to bring a kid back from the brink in ER, a hit-and-run. We spoke to the police and the kid, too, when we brought him round. Dark stuff.

I like the feel of my own sweat sliding down my torso, soaking into my shorts at the waistband. This morning I really enjoyed waking up with nothing on my body at all, and turning around to see her there in the doorway, in a see-through white dress…three seconds before I woke up all alone in the bed with a hard-on.

I can't be sure but I'm pretty sure she was jealous the other day in the parking lot, when she thought I was going out to meet a woman. Crazy. I still don't know what I think about that, which is why I let her think I *was* going on a date for a minute. Then I caved, told her I was meeting Pea. I should have just come out and told her I was meeting her because Edwina left. After getting locked out, she quite rightly said she couldn't help someone who didn't even want her there, so we have to find a new carer now. I don't know why I didn't say that to Lily, or anything, really. It feels like we're past the point of pretending with each other now...not that I know much about her ex. Something tells me there's more to that than she's letting on. I guess I don't want to seem all vulnerable and have her looking at me differently because of my past. It would only bring us closer, make me want her more, when we could never be anything more.

She's pregnant, so a fling wouldn't be fair to propose. And I don't want anything serious!

I have to admit, though, I've been thinking a little differently lately, picturing myself in the partner role instead of stuck in the friend zone.

Chicago is snowier than a Christmas movie out my windows. If it wasn't zero degrees outside I'd go running now, straight into the skyline, run Carter out of my system. I drop the weights. I've had enough. I'm tired. But if I didn't work out every day I'd go insane, especially now. How does she unravel me without even trying lately? It's not like anything could happen even if I wanted it to. She deserves forever with someone who can give it to her and the twins. I'm not a forever kind of guy and she knows that. This attraction is undoing me, the way she's been looking at me. Maybe it's all in my head?

I wipe a water splash off the counter the instant it spills, and pour hot water over a lemon from the kettle—which has never been tossed at a date by the hands of Elizabeth Montgomery.

I've asked myself if it's some strange new attraction to pregnant women, now that I'm heading for forty. Is it some deep-rooted longing to see someone raise kids the way Pea and I should've been raised, with love and respect and attention? She's twenty-four weeks pregnant, but that's almost irrelevant at this point. It's not about what she looks like, either. It's the emotions and truths coming out of her along with all of this, the way she's forcing new emotions out of me. I almost told her about Mom… I mean, I probably would have already, if I even knew where to start with it. I don't know what to do with this, wanting to keep Lily close and have her out of my way at the same time. I have to figure it out or I'll lose her.

My phone's ring slices through the silence. I snatch it from the bench, swiping to answer without checking the caller ID—a rookie mistake. My music cuts out.

"Hi, honey!"

It's Mom. She seems to be in a good mood,

but I'm instantly on edge. She talks to me, tells me she's excited to spend time with Delilah later this week, and I finally relax a little.

But in a flash her tone turns ice-cold. "Theo, while I have you, do you know how much you hurt my feelings, reminding me to take my meds? You sound like Edwina, before she abandoned me like all the others."

Here we go. My knuckles clench.

"Can we not do this right now, Mom? I've been up since dawn saving lives, and I need to unwind before tonight."

I know my tone will piss her off, especially the bit about saving lives. She never thought I'd become a doctor. It's childish, I know, but my patience with all this is at new levels of low. I'm pissed at myself for not putting my foot down sooner and insisting that something changes. Pea still doesn't want her going to some soulless facility, but at least she'd be getting round-the-clock care and not directing all this vitriol at me.

I end the call while she's still raging, right after she reminds me that she wishes I'd left when Dad did, and toss the phone aside, the screen lighting up with a missed call. I catch that it's from Lily, just as the screen goes blank again.

"Get it together." All it took was seeing her name. What is my problem?

The intercom jolts me back to reality. My heart is still hammering from the workout, never mind what Mom just said. She always knows how to hit where it hurts. It shouldn't get to me, it's her illness, I know that, but it's crippling having to hear what a terrible excuse of a son I still am to her. I shouldn't answer the door. I don't want to see anyone right now, not even the delivery guy who's bringing up my protein shakes.

When I answer, it's not the delivery guy.

"Your neighbor buzzed me in. Theo, I—" Lily cuts off. Her gaze lands on my sweat-slicked torso as she shakes snow from her coat. Her eyes widen when she sees my eyes. "What's wrong? What happened? I just tried to call you to say I was on the way…you were already on the phone."

I look at her blankly. She's my friend; why can't I tell her what just happened? She wouldn't look at me like I'm weak; surely, we're past that, I think. But she doesn't need my problems piling up on top of her own right now. "I lost track of time," I say as my inner voice chides me for being a coward, still choosing to let her see the version of Theo everyone else sees—a problem-free version that doesn't even exist right now. Then I catch her eyes on my skin, trailing downward slowly, then up again to my face. I watch her neck as she swallows, the way her cheeks change color like flowers in the sun, and damn… I'm sweaty, and I'm hardly wearing anything.

"They ran out of paint at the store," she says, clutching a giant snowy zip-up bag to her chest over her bump. I assume it holds her dress for the event tonight. "I was going to start on the nursery, which technically *was* supposed to be our yoga studio but, you know we never really use…"

She fiddles with her hair and fumbles over some words about how she needed something to do, so she figured she could help me with the other jobs if she came over early.

"Right, for the fundraiser." I clear my throat. "Come on in."

"You seem…on edge," she observes as she steps past me and takes off her coat and boots. I'd forgotten what just happened with Mom for a moment. I was thinking about dream Lily in the white dress, her hair all messed up, her lips all swollen. Her shampoo and perfume smell floats around us now as I tell her I'm fine. She looks at me like she doesn't believe me, so I make for the shower before I tell her anything at all about what my mom just said, or how she's said the same thing, about wishing I'd left with Dad, since I was ten years old.

* * *

"Theo?" Lily calls out. I'm still standing under the hot shower like I've moved to a waterfall in Hawaii. How long have I been in here?

"Yeah?" I shout back, hitting the taps off and stepping naked into the steam. Part of me wants to throw the door open and let her see me, let her want me. I could do it, force this mad attraction out into the open where we both have to address it, but I don't.

"I'm starting on those gift baskets," she says, and I can hear her lips almost up against the door. Is she teasing me now?

"Did you need a medal, some kind of reward?" I say, toweling myself off too hard. The words *gift baskets* have never sounded like such a turn-on before, which is not a great start to the day we're about to spend together.

"Very funny. I'm just telling you what I'm doing."

Telling me what she's doing? Okay, she really is teasing me. The way she looked me up and down earlier told me everything I needed to know. I've seen how women look when they want me. But she's Lily. She's being controlled by her hormones more than anything else, surely.

"If that's what you want to do, Lily, then you should do it," I say, toweling my hair and hot neck. Damn this. She doesn't need to know what

I want right now. I want to do things that would ruin both of us.

There's silence for a moment. I can hear her shuffling on the other side of the door.

"Is there something else you want to be doing, Lily?" I ask. Then I regret it. What am I initiating here? I have to cool it. Mom's wound me up. All I want to do when she gets to me is bury myself in something else to forget it. I know I've done the same to a string of women before, but I won't do that to Lily. My family's issues won't become hers, or anyone else's. Sometimes I wish I *had* left when Dad did and taken Peonie with me.

My best intentions are somewhere out the window now with the snow. Somehow, I'm inching closer to the door, my mouth by the paneling, waiting to hear her voice up close. Then it comes, in my ear.

"I want to be drinking champagne and squeezing into a hot dress, Theo. But that's not going to happen. And you really have been in there a *very* long time."

"Ri-i-i-ght." I pull a black towel around my waist and open the door. Lily jumps back and clutches her bump. The look on her face almost makes me laugh. I walk toward her in nothing but the loosely clamped towel, and she keeps on stepping backward till she's up against the bed.

"We've got loads of donations from local businesses to sort through for the baskets," I tell her. My voice comes out huskier than I was expecting, and her eyes rake over my body, up and down, then up again to my eyes. We're an inch apart. Her thigh is between my legs and she doesn't move. She just runs her gaze along the towel again, upward to my navel, till I catch her chin between my fingers. "They're near the couch, by the blinds," I tell her.

"I'll find them," she says, but her words are more a choked-up whisper. She leans softly into my fingers, then starts sinking backward to the bed, like she's on a spring, till I'm waiting for her to catapult up and fly out the door. The towel is barely masking my turn-on at this point, and she looks at my hand on it while her bottom lip quivers. I can read her face. She's not telling me to stop, but she's not laughing. This is no joke. She wants me. She came into my room and up to that door for a reason. I lower myself over her slowly, till she's pressing both hands to my flesh over my heart. She's not pushing, but somehow she's urging me closer with every breath. Everything in me screams to stop this, it's everything I said I wouldn't do with my friend, but she's driving me mad.

"I'll start organizing them," she says, right on theme, right as my knee lands between her legs.

She's flat on the bed now, lasering my eyes with hers, reaching for me.

"Make sure you categorize them by value and theme," I instruct as her fingers start to weave and tangle in my hair. She's breathing so hard I can feel it on my face. My lips are on a course to hers and I need my hands. So I release the towel.

"Theo—"

Her hands slide lower down my chest, softly across my nipples. She lets her fingers whisper inquisitively toward to my navel and I feel my own breath catch as she traces all around my thighs, across my bare backside, like she's exploring me, inch by inch, taking it all in, taking her time. I watch her face the whole time, the way she masks a gasp when she finally gets a full handful of me. I'm so hard, it's all I can do to just let her look and touch me. I lower myself farther over her, careful not to squash her, and the way she strokes and rubs me so softly, almost curiously, definitely appreciatively, almost makes me come into her palm. I roll to my back; it's the only way I can stop myself.

"What are we doing, Theo?" She's up like a flash, off the bed.

I groan, half at her, mostly at my own stupid self. "I know, I'm sorry, it's my fault, you were…"

"It's *my* fault," she counters. "I was... I don't know."

She stumbles on a shoe, almost trips over the towel I just tossed. She grasps the door handle, but not before I've caught her and spun her back to me. Her hands land against my chest as I set her right, and she tries to laugh at her misstep, even though nothing is funny right now.

"Are you okay, Carter?" I say.

She doesn't look okay. She looks like a deer in headlights now. "Yes," she assures me without moving her hands. "I just... I haven't been in a situation like this since my ex." Her words come out all fast and flustered.

"You never really told me anything about him," I say.

"I've been trying to forget," she says. "It's not you, Theo...it's me."

That old line?

I'm still naked, holding her arms, but she keeps looking over my shoulder, like she needs to escape. She reaches for the towel and hands it back to me, swipes at her eyes as I cover myself and sink back down to the bed. My heart is pounding as she leaves the room.

CHAPTER TEN

THE MOMENT THE LAST wicker basket is squeezed into the trunk, Theo slams it shut and opens the passenger door for me. I climb in past him, careful of my babies, and he leans over me to adjust the seat. I need more space than I did last time I was in his car.

I try not to breathe him in or touch him while he clicks in my seat belt. Instead, I tell him I'm perfectly capable of doing it myself, and then I wish I didn't have to find ways to mask the absolute panic I am feeling. What the hell just happened in there?

I got complete confirmation that Theo is considerably well-endowed, that's what happened. There was something about his face, though, when he let me into the apartment, like he'd just walked through hell to get to the front door. I was worried about him; it led me to him; it led to *that*. We sat there afterward, making the gift baskets for the fundraiser in the living room. I didn't kiss him. We left it all in the bedroom, didn't even bring it up. If we had kissed, I think it would have been even more intimate and way harder to come back from.

I huddle into my coat. It's a half-hour drive to the fundraising venue at the Grand Avalone Hotel. Every nerve ending feels like it's buzzing. We're going to have to talk about it; we both know it. But I don't know what I even want to say. No one told me pregnancy could make a woman so horny, even for her platonic male friends. Well, all right, the soaring levels of estrogen and progesterone, an increase in blood flow to the genitals—it's no secret all that can lead to heightened sexual desire, but this is Theo. And it's *my* blood flow that's supposed to be the issue here; *my* genitals, not his!

There's a reason he initiated it. He's a sex-mad single bachelor.

We merge onto the freeway, and that's when we hit it—a colossal traffic jam, the kind that transforms highways into parking lots and regular humans into furious honking ogres. The cars are bumper-to-bumper, horns blare through the snow. It's actually snowing again now. Theo's knuckles whiten on the steering wheel and his jaw clenches. I know he wants to wind the window down and curse at full volume out the window.

"Where's the siren when you need it?" he mutters at the windscreen, before we merge back into silence. The stillness gives me way too much room for my mind to wander. Sex with Theo *would* be amazing. And different. Grayson would never look into my eyes, or invite me to explore him slowly and erotically like Theo just did. It was like he gave up all desire to actually connect with me, until I started fearing connection. I was scared of it, scared of doing something wrong, scared of being belittled or rejected or both. It was so warped and twisted, the mind games!

That back there with Theo, though. That was…

"This is bad, isn't it, Carter?" Theo says.

My insides rearrange themselves at the sound of his voice. "It's a little awkward, yes—"

"I didn't think the traffic would be this bad."

Oh, he means the traffic. "It's not your fault." I force a smile. "At least the chocolates won't melt. If this was a summer ball situation, it would be a different story."

"I have a story to make this traffic jam more interesting," he says, before launching into a tale about Delilah as a toddler and a story he would read to her about a mouse princess and a grasshopper prince and a dragon. I guess we're still not going to address what happened in his bedroom.

"Good thing this princess brought her ball

gown to change into," I say, more to distract my-self from his mouth than anything. I wanted to kiss him all afternoon. I'm glad I didn't. Sort of.

"And your prince here still has his stallion waiting patiently," he replies, deadpan except for the smirk, tapping his fingers against the wheel.

The sound exits my mouth before I can form words, something between a snort and a squeal. "Did you just refer to your penis as a stallion?"

"We were working to a theme. Princes ride horses!"

"I get it," I tell him, and thank goodness we're laughing. It feels good.

"Listen," he says, and my stomach flips as his tone turns serious. "I'm really sorry if I made things weird."

Silence. I can barely gather my thoughts enough to answer. "I…um…" I turn to him, will-ing myself to be honest.

Tell him you wanted it, my devil voice screams.

"I don't think we have to analyze it, really, do we?" I say instead and he nods at the road ahead, tapping his fingers to the wheel.

I'm a coward. I don't know why I told him that. I *want* to analyze it now. I just don't want it to seem like I expect anything, or need any-thing. This is uncomfortable. And there's an-other pressing issue now, too—one that simply cannot wait out a traffic jam. "Theo…" I begin, shifting in my seat. "I really need to use the bathroom."

His eyes flicker to mine and he frowns. "Here? Now?"

"Blame the babies," I say. "They're pressing all sorts of buttons."

"I know better buttons."

"Stop it, Theo!"

"Okay, okay. Let me think." His gaze scans the vicinity along with mine. We're probably looking at an impossible situation. There's so much snow and concrete and cars.

"I don't think the babies care about traffic laws anymore, Grasshopper Prince," I tell him. "Summon your dragon. Find us a way."

He salutes me dramatically. "I will not fail you, Mouse Princess."

I'm laughing, but I wish I weren't because it makes me need to pee even more. I clutch the handle as he edges us toward the shoulder, inching past the honks and a thousand glares until we are safely—sort of—out of the direct line of traffic.

"Privacy is going to be a little bit of an issue here, Carter." He turns to rummage through the back seat and I warn my fingers not to touch him again. "But I think I found my dragon."

He pulls out the oversize fundraising banner that Delilah's friends made and I feel my eyes grow to the size of satellites. "I can't pee behind this…it's got pictures of kids on it."

"They're pictures, Lily."

"It says *Together for a Healthier Tomorrow* on it, Theo. There's nothing healthy about me peeing behind it on the highway."

"Do you need to go or not?" Quickly, he drapes the banner from the door and beckons me forward. It's the side farthest from the on-coming traffic, so I guess no one will see, but honestly, do I even have a choice? I'm bursting.

I hold my bump as the freezing wind and snow blows around my legs, and Theo creates a makeshift stall, instructing me to squat.

"This is so undignified," I tell him.

His eyes shine with something wicked before he turns his back, and if I didn't have to pee and safeguard two tiny humans inside me I might pull him down on top of me. This is weirdly ex-hilarating actually, but, oh, Lord, I am already a terrible mother.

"Make it quick, Carter, and try not to pee on your boots."

I manage the quickest roadside relief in his-tory while Theo stands guard, humming the theme song to some eighties action movie. It is quite ridiculous. And exactly why I'm feeling all this about him. I never really saw our con-nection for what it is before. We have something rare, I think. It's friendship but it's also trust and respect and fun, and being there when you really, really have to pee. He still hasn't told me what's really going on with his mom, though. He still doesn't trust me *enough* to tell me anything, even when I ask. What is it that he's so afraid to talk about, I wonder? What don't I know, besides the fact that he doesn't seem to be as big of a playboy as I thought, lately. He could have brought anyone here today, but he chose to bring me. He also chose to open that door, drop that towel…

"Mission accomplished?" he asks as I emerge from behind the banner with what remains of my dignity.

"Your gallantry knows no bounds," I retort, while the fact that I'm wondering things I've never wondered about this mad, intriguing, infuriating, talented, unpredictable man takes on new shapes and forms and colors in my head until I miss his next words completely. "What did you say?"

He rolls the banner back up and puts it in the back seat. "I said I'm going to auction off this banner when it comes to raising funds for your maternity leave party. You've put a dent in its value, but we should still be able to secure some supermarket flowers."

"I hope you tell them a princess used it."

We drive on and talk about work and I'm so glad some of the weirdness has gone. I shouldn't try to sweep what happened under the carpet, though. Even if he doesn't romanticize or analyze sexual encounters like I do, it doesn't mean what's going on isn't real for him, too.

His phone blasts more Taylor Swift. He mutters "Delilah…" as he hits the decline button.

"You hung up on Delilah?"

"No, she put Taylor as my ringtone and I keep meaning to… Never mind."

The phone is relentless. It rings again almost immediately. "Come on, Theo, answer it. We're stuck here, anyway." I push the call through to the speaker without waiting for his consent.

"Theo!" The female voice that explodes around us makes me physically jump. Theo's arm comes up across my chest like he's expecting this woman to appear in the windscreen.

"Mom," he says, a forced calmness in his voice.

"Do not cut me off again! How dare you…?"

My hands go to my bump as she carries on ranting. She goes on and on, yelling, crying, so much emotion, so much vitriol, and it's hurtful, horrible. I think she's intoxicated, too. The things she says to him make my heart pound with so much secondhand embarrassment for him and pity for *her*, that I can't look at him anymore. He sees my face.

"Mom, I'm driving." Finally, he cuts her off.

"Theo, the things she said… She sounds like she…"

"Like she hates me."

I stare at him, shaking my head. "Like she needs some serious help. Why didn't you tell me it was this bad?"

"Well. Now you know." He presses his lips into a line and swallows back whatever he's trying to say but I know what he needs. He's stressed and embarrassed over whatever his mom's suffering from, and he needs space for his thoughts, and he also needs me not to press him.

Finally, we pull up to the venue. "All right, let's get this over with, Princess Mouse," he says.

I put a hand to his arm and he lets out a sigh from somewhere deeper than his bones. "I'm here, if you want to talk," I say.

"I thought we weren't analyzing it."

"Not about us, Theo."

"So there's an us, Lily?"

"No, there is no us. Stop it."

His eyes don't leave my lips and I see the way he stops himself from leaning in to kiss me. It happens in a fraction of a second, and in that fraction of a second his eyes sweep up over mine and I swear I feel like I could melt right into the seat, despite all the snow outside. I swear he wants to melt into me, too, if only so we can both take some of his pain away. I see how his jaw shifts as his tongue moves behind his lips; how he lowers his eyes then pulls away until the connection is broken.

The moment passes like it never happened. He pops the trunk and slides out of the car.

For a moment I'm truly shocked that he didn't just kiss me. Or that I didn't kiss him. Then I have to laugh at myself and my open mouth and my racing heartbeat. This is how he does it. He's such a goddamn tease, such a good flirt. Really, truly, the best I've ever had to face. He wipes my brain of everything else, and I love it. When I'm not freaking out about it, I love how playing with him makes me feel. Grayson never... not even before he changed and sucked my soul dry. It was nothing like this. But Theo is hurting, too. I see him clearer now than I ever have. How long has his mom been acting like this?

A guy arrives to help unload the baskets, and Theo greets him with his trademark high-five shoulder bump. He only ever does that when he really likes someone, which now that I think about it is only maybe this guy and my dad. He truly must be going through hell in secret if he gets treated like that by his own mother. He could have been on the phone to her when I arrived at his place earlier. Maybe *that* was why he looked like his psyche had just taken a bullet. What I witnessed in the car was a continuation of her tirade, which was probably one of many, if his reactions to my questions are anything to go by. I'm not going to let this go. The woman clearly has some kind of mental disorder, maybe alcoholism or bipolar disorder. Why is she not getting treatment?

"This place is something else," I say, attempting to take a basket from him as the valet drives off with the Porsche and we crunch across the snowy gravel. He refuses to let me carry anything, even though he's balancing the banner over his shoulder along with the bag containing my dress. "Let me help," I say as we step over the threshold. He grunts a no, then ignores me.

The entrance hall is like a film set with its splendor. The chandeliers sparkle over us as I walk beside him across the checkered floor. People are milling about already, placing welcome glasses on special tall stands. I tell him I want a grand staircase like the one here, someday. It sweeps up to the second floor in a marble dance toward the domed ceiling. From somewhere the strains of a string quartet meet my ears. A tingle creeps along my arms and I catch Theo looking at me.

"You look cute in an opulent setting. Did I ever tell you that?" he says, heading for the staircase. "I should've switched McFadden's for more fancy establishments sooner. Looking at your face is almost worth the parking fee."

"Oh, you're good," I say, but I'm already thinking about my dress, how I wish on this one night I didn't have a bump to squeeze into it. I catch myself and curse. I didn't mean that. Gosh, I'm awful. I didn't mean that.

He's lugging the banner up the stairs beside me suddenly, and I try to take the other end of it.

"You didn't wash your hands, remember," he says, moving it out of my reach.

I laugh. We both know I didn't get pee on it, but he's making it a thing. "You're the one touching it, Theo!"

"I need to wash it, and you need to wash your hands. And your mouth."

"Why would I wash my mouth? You didn't kiss me."

We're at the top of the spiral steps now, the mounting crowds bustling beneath us. Theo props the banner against the railings and turns to face me. Stepping to my toes, he leans in so close I can feel his lips brush my neck when he speaks, and my heart shoots up to the very spot where his breath warms my skin, till it's thudding in my ears.

"Did you want me to kiss you? Did you want to carry on with what we started in the apartment?"

Someone sweeps past us. My heart is hammering now.

"I think you did," he says. "So did I. We both know I want you, I'm not denying that, but we also both know I won't be good for you, Lily. You were the one who stopped it and I think you were right to."

"I did stop it," I manage. "And I have all kinds of reasons. But I'm more concerned about you, if I'm honest. You're being abused. That's what it sounds like."

A darkness crosses his face. "She's my mother."

"I know what abuse sounds like, Theo. It doesn't matter where it comes from."

A storm is raging in his head. I can see it in his eyes. I draw a breath, and I'm surprised at the emotion that escapes when I speak, the way my voice cracks. "I promised myself that tonight would be perfect. We were meant to escape together, Theo, have some fun, and you know what? Even stopping for that emergency pee was more fun than I've had in ages, but…"

I falter suddenly, closing my mouth. I can't stop thinking how Grayson took so much away from me for so long, drained the fun-loving side of me clean away. I let him do that. And now

Theo's mother's condition is putting his own mental health in jeopardy.

"Don't let this illness of hers take over your life, too. She needs help," I finish. Theo just scowls at the floor, then at me.

"You don't know the half of what's going on," he says eventually.

"Because you've chosen not to tell me," I counter, forcing my anger below the surface. I'm mad because I didn't press him enough sooner, and because he's shut me out. "You've chosen not to tell me! Look, Theo, I was a victim of abuse for a long time, and it completely sucked the life out of me, so yes, I kind of want to know that she's getting help, and I really want to know that *you* are okay, too."

Theo stares at me. His eyes are a million questions, all layering up in the blue, multiplying as he processes what I've just said. "What are you telling me?"

"Grayson," I say. Just vocalizing his name makes me rub my arms against a sudden chill.

"What did he do to you?"

I can hear the hurt in his voice, the confusion. My mind keeps spinning over and over. He asks me again through his teeth what he did to me, and I can feel the heat between us burning something down. "It wasn't physical," I tell him. It wasn't; it was worse. I can feel my shutters coming up now, and Theo's, too. This is not how I wanted this night to go.

"How long were you with him?"

"Four years," I tell him. "We need some space."

His eyebrows shoot up incredulously. "Us? Here? How will that even be poss—?"

"Figure it out, Grasshopper."

I leave him at the top of the stairs and try not to fall over. I shouldn't hurt Theo. He's being hurt enough by this situation with his family, but yes, it's what Grayson did to me, and when Theo shuts me out it brings it all back; the way I felt alone, surrounded by people. I was so alone, always, and *I'm* still hurting, too.

CHAPTER ELEVEN

OF COURSE WE'RE seated next to each other. For hours she's avoided me, talking to this person and that person and ignoring me, even when I purposefully pulled a face at her while I was stringing the banner up across the banisters.

She's impervious to my charms as I pull her seat out at the table, and she doesn't look at me, even as she slides in next to me. "Thank you, Doctor Montgomery," she says coolly, for the sake of the eight other important people around the table.

"It's good to see you after all this time, Doctor Carter," I try, but she doesn't crack.

All right, so I should have told her sooner about what exactly is wrong with Mom, before she was forced to hear it for herself. But she knows now, some of it at least, and I'm more torn up about what she told *me*. She was with a guy for four years who had zero respect or appreciation for what he had right in front of him, who *abused* her in some way? I don't know the details and she probably doesn't want to tell me, but how have I never known this? How has she never told me she was in an abusive relationship? I feel helpless, angry for her, even though I know it's in the past.

She does look hot in that dress, though. The color of the trees in spring, all sparkly with lace crisscross stitches and matching green earrings that people might say bring out her eyes. Her eyes don't need enhancing in my opinion. I kind of like it when they burn me.

I arrange my napkin on my knee. She mirrors me, so I tap my foot to hers. She tuts and moves it, so I tap it again until finally, she cracks a smile. Just a flicker but it's there behind her Ice Queen agenda. She picks up her fork and I can't *not* see it again… Her hands all over me before we left the house, her eyes burning into mine, wanting me. I never once touched her. I didn't need to… She was doing it all on her own and she loved it. Right until she didn't—she ended up with her ex in her head. Grayson. I swear I'll run an ambulance over him *and* leave the scene without him.

Dr. Robert Simmons, widely regarded as one of the best cardiothoracic surgeons in the country, has dedicated his career to the intricate field of heart and lung surgery, and he is absolutely loving that everyone knows it. He fills her glass with sparkling water as he talks and I ignore my phone vibrating in my suit pocket. I watch her mouth as she listens politely to the doctor's story, pecking at a bread roll. We didn't kiss yet; her mouth never touched me. I don't know how we managed that at my place, or earlier in the car, but I don't want to treat her like some dispensable item I can use and cast aside. I won't.

I can't resist a real beer. Lily eats her salad like a bird when it appears, nodding in all the right places as Simmons reminds us all how he attended Johns Hopkins University "back in the good old days." She still barely looks at me. I carve into my steak, only half tasting it. From somewhere across the room I hear my name mentioned. Two female execs are whispering, looking right at me.

Lily whispers to me…actually it's more like a cat from a cartoon: sultry, seductive, with the perfect amount of spite. "Don't you want to go over there, Theo? Remind them how being with you is a terrible idea? Or don't you say that to one-night stands?"

"Oh, so you've decided to grace me with your words now, have you, Princess?" I smirk. She's pissed about what I said, when I told her I'd be no good for her. She knows I'm right, but her pride took a hit, and who knows what else that Grayson guy put into her head? A lot more things are starting to make sense about Carter now.

I catch her looking at the execs again over my shoulder. I should make a point of going over there just to wind her up, but what would that achieve? She's the one I want now, even if there's stuff we *both* don't particularly want to discuss. I press a hand to hers under the table, holding it against her bare knee, and twist my chair to hers. "Let's go somewhere and talk, Lily."

She puts her fork down calmly. "I'm eating my salad."

I run my hand along her inner thigh, softly, slowly, till she hides the smallest moan behind her hand and swipes me away like a pesky fly. "We'll get pizza on the way home," I say.

"What makes you think I'm getting back in a car with you?"

I lean in closer, whispering into her ear. "Because I'm the only one who will untie that banner up there. And bring it back downstairs through *all* these people. And put it in the car and make a shelter for you with it when you need to stop. I am the *only* person who will do that, Carter. Come with me."

She pushes my hand away. "Don't tell me what to do."

"Okay, this is stupid. Seriously." I take her

hand back and hold it tighter to her knee. "Don't compare me to him," I tell her before she can pull away from me. "I don't know what he did to you, Lily, but you know I'd never hurt you."

Her eyes gloss over as she looks away. Then Dr. Simmons's scratchy beard appears over her shoulder and she almost leaps off her seat into my lap.

"Forgive me if I'm stepping out of line here, but did you say your partner wasn't here tonight?"

I scratch my chair loudly as I reposition my seat. Oh, this will be good.

Lily sniffs and then scratches her chair just as loudly to face him. "My partner?"

"The father of your child?" Dr. Simmons presses, and I don't miss his eyes moving to me. This is amusing me more than it should.

"What makes you think that my *partner* is also the father of my babies?" Lily says next, and a woman at the table presses her hands together, addressing us all.

"Why *do* men think they can probe us like this?" she asks, like we've just sat down for her TED Talk. I see now that she's pregnant, too, and she's also here alone. Oh, this is going better than I expected. I hope someone's filming.

It's finally Dr. Simmons's turn to speak, but unfortunately he's cut short, because a huge commotion is breaking out across the room.

A man. Middle-aged. He's staggering from his chair, clutching his chest over his suit. His face is contorted in pain. I can see the sweat beading on his forehead from here.

"Stay here," I tell Lily as I stand, but of course she gets right up after me, gathering up her dress.

"He's having a heart attack. Call emergency," I bark at the nearest onlooker, a woman who fumbles with her phone in a panic.

There are other doctors here amongst the sponsors but Lily and I synchronize, largely without words, as the room fades into the background. All that matters is the man gasping for air on the floor. I check his pulse and order others to clear the space.

"Sir, can you hear me?" Lily asks him.

"His breathing is shallow. We need to start CPR," I say as someone mentions a defib stored downstairs. We work together, counting compressions and giving rescue breaths. It's strange how everything else disappears when the world is narrowed down to the task of keeping someone alive.

The AED is here now, hustled over to us by Dr. Simmons, and in seconds I'm cutting off his shirt and lining up the pads. "Clear!"

I brace myself, letting another jolt out. This is not how this gentleman must have thought this evening would go. His losing this battle would destroy his wife, who's staring at all this and shaking like she's never been more afraid in her whole life. Then…

"Carter, we've got a pulse."

I can already hear the sirens outside.

The paramedics filter in and I step back with Lily. I reach for her hand as he's carried away on a stretcher. If I'm exhausted after that, Lily must be ready to drop. She won't let me take her hand.

"I can take you home if you want?" I tell her, just as the MC hops onto the stage and announces that we've done all we can for the moment, and the show must go on. Of course, what else would they say? We have a hospital to fund. The band starts up, and people start filtering to the dance floor.

"You should dance," Lily tells me, lowering herself to a seat. "Go find those execs."

"I'm not going to do that, Carter."

"Do it."

"Don't tell me what to do," I tell her, and she rolls her eyes.

"Touché."

It's not long before I'm lured to the dance floor, anyway, and I don't even know why I stay on it, following her orders. What is wrong with me? But I do like watching her turn away every single man who approaches her; even the attractive ones who might possibly be single. I wait maybe ten minutes before returning, and she cocks an eyebrow.

"Dance with me?" I say, holding out my hand. "I assume you have now washed your hands."

"That's the least romantic thing anyone has ever said to me. Thank you, I won't be doing that."

She stands, anyway, when I put my hand down to her, but I can see the weight of her thoughts in her eyes. I cup her chin again. "You can stand on my feet if you're tired," I say, but her expression almost breaks me. This is not the time to make light of anything. I curse my bad habit of deflecting discomfort with humor.

"I'm sorry," I tell her. "I'm sorry about what happened at my place, how you found out about Mom, it's a lot. And your ex. But you know I'd never hurt you."

"Not on purpose, maybe, but I'm pregnant, Theo," she announces as if it's not blatantly obvious. She lowers her head and sighs at the floor. "You were right before. This wouldn't be a good thing to explore…"

"I wasn't hitting on you!"

"But you want to. You admitted it. I have to think about my babies."

I close my mouth. She sighs heavily again, and I force myself not to say a thing. Kissing in her mind leads to commitment, and the fact that I can't offer it, and I should let it go. Except my mind is going to the exact same place—if I kiss her, I'll want more, and this isn't me. At least it didn't used to be. She's messing with my head.

"When I walked into your place earlier," she says, "you looked like you had the weight of the world on your shoulders. Was it your mom then, too?"

I nod solemnly. So she guessed that?

My phone vibrates in my pocket. It's the hospital with the update we've been waiting for. "Doctor Montgomery, good news. The patient you sent over is stable and recovering well."

"Thank you," I breathe out. "Thanks for the update."

Someone hears and wants me up on the stage. I tell Lily to wait where she is. This conversation isn't over. "I'll drive you home. To your place."

"I'm serious, Theo, I want to go on my own. I really think we need some space."

I'm ushered onto the stage, where the MC hands me the mic. I tell the crowd our man is stable and he is going to be just fine, and the room erupts and decides it's the perfect time for the gift basket auction. Lily's eyes find mine across the applause. She's standing in the doorway now, holding her coat. By the time I've made my way through the throng of people and out into the snowy open air, she's gone.

CHAPTER TWELVE

WE WORK THROUGH the days now, avoiding each other for the most part. Theo does his thing and I do mine, and when we have to work together at the hospital, we're polite and efficient but it doesn't go beyond that. For almost two months, as my belly's grown bigger and my body more tired, I've refused to let it. But I have thought about the fundraiser every single day since.

What happened in his bedroom plays over and over and over in my dreams. The memories only make my already crazy hormones fire into over-drive. It wasn't right how we left things. He shut me down, then I shut *him* down, and now we're at an impasse. I had to shut him down, though. Things were getting too complicated. I'm about to give birth, and my days are about to be nothing but babies...more babies than usual and that is a lot.

At thirty-one weeks, I'm even bigger now than I thought my body could possibly get. Beach ball doesn't cover it. I feel like there's a baby elephant curled up inside me.

I walk around my little patients, all sleeping so peacefully in their incubators. I reach through to one of them, gently stroking the fingers of Baby Jay, another preemie barely weighing two pounds. He is one of the most fragile in our unit. He had a heart operation just a few days ago.

"Doctor Montgomery is the biggest charmer in Chicago. Do you think he would've taken me seriously?" I tell the tiny infant. "And if we really had…done some wicked things that only adults do…he only would have made light of it afterward. Then where would we be?"

The baby's innocent face scrunches up adorably, like he understands. But even I don't understand. I'm saying all these things about Theo every day, mostly in my head, but I don't always believe them. I miss him making me laugh, the way we forged a real, undeniable connection through all the recent chaos, and maybe that's what scares me the most. He told me he would never hurt me. I fell into his eyes when he said that, in a room full of all those people. I truly, honestly believed him. Then that poor man had a heart attack and everything went crazy, and my mind made a huge deal of *everything* that happened, and the only way out was to set fire to it all and run. I did the right thing, though, didn't I?

Baby Jay blinks and crinkles up his tiny eyes and mouth. I adjust his tube and press my palm to the incubator. "I told him I needed space and he's only being respectful by giving me it. Truthfully, I think I'm afraid of liking someone too much after my last relationship was such a mess. I can't afford to lose myself to another guy, or to anything. I have my babies to think about."

The infant gurgles at me softly, fixing me with his big brown eyes. He gets it, I can tell. I can't help but huff a laugh as I give his hand one last gentle stroke. I tell him I hope my own babies are such good listeners. And then I realize someone is standing in the doorway.

"Theo. You snuck up on me again. Why do you do that?"

"I'm on a break. Sorry, can't help my tiny, silent footsteps," he says, before stomping heavily toward me with a completely straight face. Somehow, his shoes still barely make a sound on the floor.

"Did I order a clown in here?" I ask him, but I can't fight the start of a laugh as it bubbles up, damn him. Then he steps dramatically carefully and quietly forward to check on Baby Jay, and my heart does a somersault at the forced proximity. I never know if it's going to be another weird, awkward silence lately, or if we're actually going to have a conversation. Is it bad that even though I asked for space, I can still picture every inch of him naked?

I adjust the tiny knit cap on another infant, searching for something to ask him. But it's Theo's voice that breaks the silence, and of course my traitorous heart leaps when he casts his blue eyes to me.

"I actually did seek you out for a reason." He follows me as I walk to the end of the incubators. I get a lungful of his cologne, just how his bedroom smelled. Exactly how he smelled when he carried me out of McFadden's in the worst possible scenario that may or may not have intensified a mounting crush on my friend. The cologne no longer makes me nauseated, that's long gone, but it makes me think bad thoughts that I promised myself I would never think again.

"Should I be scared of this reason?" I ask him.

"It's about tomorrow."

I stiffen slightly. I just *know* what he's about to say before he says it. "What about tomorrow?"

"Your maternity leave celebration. I can't make it." His gaze holds something like an apology, but it doesn't mask the flicker of something else—regret, maybe? Guilt. I won't show how disappointed I am; it's not like we've even been speaking lately.

"So much for raising money by selling the

banner," I say instead. The pangs from his rejection make me shuffle in place.

"I decided to keep that for myself, for the memories, you know." He lowers his voice, brushes my shoulder with his as he leans in. "I put it up on the ceiling, over my bed."

"Hilarious," I tell him.

I hate that I like the way he does this, switches so casually between joking with me as a friend and reminding me that he's clearly still thinking about that moment when we blurred the lines. He must know I'm still thinking about it, too. Before he can elaborate on why exactly he can't make it to my gathering, if he was even going to, his phone distracts him and I catch a glimpse of the caller ID—his mom. Again. He's programmed her name to come up as "Just be kind!"

I shouldn't feel sidelined by the persistent intrusion of his family drama; that wouldn't be fair. I can see how he's sick of it, too. It's all over his face. He doesn't want to look at his phone all the time, especially not here, but he can't help it; he feels like he has to. Like I always gave myself a minimum of three rings before I picked up to Grayson. If I took any longer than that to pick up he would simmer on it and bring it up later, accusing me of being too busy for him, which of course I was most of the time. I work at a hospital.

Just how bad is his mother's condition, whatever it is? After that call I overheard in the car, I haven't been able to stop thinking about it, and how much it all just reminds me of being stuck under Grayson's thumb.

Theo writes a text, and I watch his face as he shoves the phone back into his coat.

"So, we *are* trying to get help for my mother," he finally says, but his eyes dart away and he dashes his hands through his hair. "We have an appointment at a place tomorrow. It's taken two months for a spot to come up."

"A place?" It's the vaguest response from him on a serious matter that I think I've ever had. "Do you want to tell me more?" I encourage, but the Taylor Swift ringtone cuts me off this time. It's very quiet, and he doesn't startle the babies, but it's a melody that is still far too upbeat for this moment.

"You really need to change that," I tell him, and he replies that I need to show him how, exactly, before he excuses himself to talk to Peonie. There is always something with him. Every time he takes a break and turns his phone on, it's a flood. How can he handle all that on top of his job? I turn my attention back to the little fighter in the incubator. Just looking at these infants makes it even more real that two little lives will soon turn my entire world upside down. And with everything being so crazy, I still haven't gotten around to painting the yoga room. Rose agreed that it should become the nursery, and we finally got the paint delivered from the store, but that's about as far as we've got.

Theo steps back into the room. "So, the place?" I ask him.

He nods, folds his arms across his perfectly ironed coat like he's putting up a safety barrier all of a sudden. "It's called Serenity Pines. They specialize in DBT."

"Dialectical Behavior Therapy," I add. I know about this a little at least. It's commonly used in more individualized cases of depression. It tackles the extreme emotional thoughts that exist in severe cases. He tells me he's been trying to get her help for years beyond a revolving door of caretakers who come to her house and wind up leaving soon after, but that she doesn't think she needs it, and I can tell this is having a huge emotional impact on him. I feel so guilty now that I haven't been around for him, that we've been stuck avoiding each other like this. I'm the one who's been selfish.

"It must be a relief, knowing she might finally get some help," I say. He still has his arms folded over his coat like a barrier. Is it wrong that I want to hug him now and tell him things will be all right? "I don't know the half of it, like you said at the fundraiser, but it seems like something you've been wanting to fix for a while," I add.

"Yes, but it's not just down to me. It's complicated," he says, and he turns to one of the incubators now, moves some tubes, and the silence stretches between us. I'm not going to push him for more information now. This is more than he's ever said about the whole situation, so that's something. He's been trying to get help for two months, which means our blowup at the fundraiser made some impact. I'm actually proud that I might have helped in some way. It's already more than I managed to do for myself when I needed it.

"So, what's been going on with you?" he asks eventually, changing the subject. He draws the last word out as he sidles closer to me. "How is everything in baby world?"

"A lot, and they're not even here yet," I say. Then, because we're here and he's asking, I tell him how I still need to get car seats and paint the nursery but I don't even have a ladder or any paintbrushes yet.

"I assume we're *not* going for pink and blue?" he says. "Someone like you…you picked a glitter paint, didn't you?"

I smile and tell him most certainly not on both accounts, and then he digs his hand in his other pocket and pulls out an envelope. He holds it out with purpose and I stare at it. "This is for me?"

"Just a little something, because I'm missing your thing," he says.

"A peace offering, you mean?"

"Just open it." He's trying to be casual, like he gives me little gifts every day or something, but I can tell by the way he watches me open the envelope that he's nervous about giving this to me. It's why he came in here to find me in the first place.

I pull out a voucher for a massage and a facial treatment at a place in my neighborhood I've never been to called Elysian Wellness Spa. It's for two people. He tells me how it has a salt pool float that's specially designed to ease the weight of pregnancy, and three different mud baths, and if I'm good I might even get some jasmine tea.

"I thought you and Rose could go," he says.

I hold it to my chest. "Theo, this is… I don't know what to say."

"There's nothing *to* say. Just go and relax."

He looks at me a moment too long, just a little too close, and I can feel everything we started the day of the fundraiser taking up the space between us all over again. "Lily," he starts, and I can tell he's going to say something serious. "I know you said you needed space, and I respect that, it's smart. So you don't get all magnetized to me again…"

"You flatter yourself."

"I've been thinking a lot about what you said, about Grayson," he continues.

My shoulders tense and I sniff at him.

"Four years, isn't that what you said? I can't get my head around it, Carter. How did I not know?"

"I don't tell you everything, Theo, the same as you don't tell me everything. Anyway, it's in the past," I say quickly, and before I even have the chance to tell him why just the mention of Grayson sends my blood levels through the roof, the sudden blare of a monitor alarm cuts in. Theo's head snaps up. His eyes dart to the incubator at the other end of the room.

"Baby Jay," he says, and I follow him quickly. Baby Jay was just fine! I tell him so, but something's wrong now, very wrong. His chest is rising and falling erratically beneath the translucent incubator. His skin has turned a frightening mottled purple in parts, and his little fingers keep clutching for an invisible lifeline as Theo checks his levels.

"It's okay, Carter, you've got this."

"Oxygen's dropping," I say. I can't seem to stop my fingers from trembling as I adjust the flow of oxygen. "Help me, please."

Somehow, my foggy brain knows where to take my feet and hands. Theo places the oxygen mask over the baby's face, while I prep an intubation kit. Baby Jay is still struggling for breath. This is breaking my heart.

"Pipe," I tell him, and I hand him a tiny endotracheal tube, which he slides deftly into place and secures swiftly with the surgical tape I hand him next. I'm actually shaking. This should not be happening...we were watching him!

"I was watching him," I tell Theo now, and he presses a calming hand to mine.

"Breathe," he says. The warning flickering in his eyes sends me back to silence. He's right, I'm getting too emotional. I'm taking this too personally, and he's reminding me of that, whilst also being my rock. God, I've missed him. But this is not supposed to be happening.

Finally, after what feels like hours, but is likely only a few minutes, Baby Jay's heart rate stabilizes and his breathing grows less frantic. I'm so emotional now, though. It feels like everything is piling up on top of me and I'm pretty sure Theo's bringing up Grayson is contributing to it. Grayson's left a mark on everything and if I don't watch my step, the way he haunts me will haunt my babies, too.

Theo catches me in the corridor. "What happened in there, Carter?" He frowns.

"It got on top of me, I'm sorry."

He sighs at me, takes me by the elbow and walks me down the corridor. "Don't apologize," he says. "You're pregnant. You're allowed to be emotional."

I nod and smooth down my coat, and I tell him thank God I'm about to go on maternity leave because I'd hate for anyone here to see me crack the way he just did. He asks if he can do anything, and if I want to talk about everything. The hope in his eyes ties my stomach into a knot for a thousand reasons and I tell him no.

"I can't, I'm really busy."

He bobs his head, looks away and I can feel the walls coming straight back up again. I want to hear more about Serenity Pines. I know it's selfish not to ask, but it's always been like drawing blood from a stone. Who knows if he'd even tell me what he's been through to get to this point? "You've been drip-feeding information for months, Theo, and now you want to talk?"

"Better late than never," he says. He wants to ask me more about Grayson, too, I can feel it, and I feel sick just thinking about how he'll look at me when he discovers all the crap I put up with before leaving.

"I can't do this right now, I'm sorry," I say, and I hate how disappointed he looks, but I need to start sticking to my boundaries. I need to focus on my babies. I tell him thanks again for the spa day. I tell him I hope it goes well at Serenity Pines, and then I excuse myself. I don't see him again for over a week.

CHAPTER THIRTEEN

"UNCLE THEO, do we have any orange juice left?" Delilah has just emerged from her room, rubbing her eyes. Taylor Swift smiles at me from the back of her pajama top, which reminds me—I still need to change that damn ringtone.

"Bottom shelf, behind the milk," I reply, going back to flipping my omelets. She stayed over after I took her to a show last night, but Pea's picking her up to go shopping soon. My head is all over the place as Delilah talks to me, and I feel bad that I can't really focus on what she's saying. I keep reflecting on that disaster of a first appointment at Serenity Pines.

We eat mostly in silence until Delilah puts down her fork. I watch the frown line her forehead when she tells me she misses Lily. "Where is she?"

"Maternity leave," I tell her, pushing my food around on my plate. I should be starving after my workout but there's too much on my mind. They only take new patients at Serenity every few months, so we had to wait, and when that new intake appointment came up on the same day as Lily's leaving thing, what was I supposed to do? As it was, Mom reluctantly agreed to check the place out, but freaked out at the last minute. She made a huge scene outside the car before we'd even left the city, got a cop sprinting over to see how we were "hurting her," which obviously, we were not. Pea and I had to go alone to the facility and talk to them.

"Did you do something to upset Lily?" Delilah's question catches me off guard. She waggles her finger at me. "You did, didn't you? What did you do?"

"What makes you think I did anything?" I say, though admittedly, she's probably right. I've kept my distance from Carter. It hasn't been easy, I hope the spa voucher wasn't pushing it, but I think I'm getting a clearer idea of why our hookup…our almost-hookup…was some kind of defining boundary line for her. She's been through it. This Grayson guy put her through it. The fact that she's about to become a mother has her on high alert. I don't blame her for thinking I'd run a mile from her if she gave me an inch, and I know my reputation doesn't help with her trust issues. Especially when I'm still keeping things from her.

"She was around a lot, and then she wasn't. I miss her," Delilah says again.

"I miss her, too," I tell her, taking a dishcloth to a piece of egg right as it falls off her plate. I *do* miss her. It's been strange at the hospital, not seeing her around. I've seen Rose, obviously, in the cafeteria, on the rare occasion she breaks away from the tight-knit bubble that constitutes the Fertility Department upstairs. She told me they still haven't painted that damn nursery.

Lily being on mat leave only makes me think about her more. She was the one who finally got me to push Pea into doing something about Mom. I didn't think Pea would agree, she never has before, but I think she saw the emotional impact it's had on me, on top of all the stuff with Lily.

"Are you going to see her today?" Delilah presses. "It's Saturday."

"Why are you so invested?" I ask her, and she looks at me like I'm crazy, tells me Lily is—and I quote—"the only one who gives me hope that maybe my uncle won't be alone forever."

Sassy, but for a girl turning twelve next month she's more clued into things than I ever was. Her words rattle around in my head long after Pea's collected her, till I find myself in the garage, hauling a ladder and all the painting supplies I own to my car.

* * *

"Theo?" Lily answers the door in surprise, one hand resting on the curve of her belly. Her eyes trail along the ladder over my shoulder and the buckets at my feet. "The auditions for shirtless decorator were last week," she says through a tight smile.

"What makes you think I'll be taking my shirt off?" I reply as Jasper appears and starts curling around my ankles. "I charge sixty bucks an hour and my clothes stay on. Do we have a deal?"

Her lip puckers under her teeth as she fights another smile and steps aside. The cat weaves around us like he's daring me to drop my tools as Lily leads me to what will soon be the twins' nursery. I set down the ladder and force my hands not to swipe at the cat hair I know will be all over my jeans. She pads around barefoot and cracks open a window. It's cold as hell outside but we're going to need the air. I need air already.

She's always been hot, but pregnancy seems to have transformed her into some ethereal creature these past couple months. Her hair is loose and shiny around her face. The maternity dress is a pink I've never seen on her, a feminine print with tiny white flowers.

We make small talk about the attendees at her leaving party while we both try to ignore how we're enclosed in a small space, and how Rose isn't home. Should I have come over here? She didn't tell me to leave, I guess, and she really does need help with this.

"I didn't expect you, Theo." She glances behind me now, presumably at my car parked out front, then meets my eyes.

"And I didn't expect to be here," I admit. "But Delilah…"

"Delilah?"

"Never mind," I say, making for the three cans of paint in the corner. The room is bare except for two cribs and a changing table, and they've gone as far as putting a plastic sheet across the floor at least. "So, what's the color?"

"Sunset blush," Lily answers, stepping close as I crouch to my haunches and inspect the paint. "Warm and neutral, not overly girly. No glitter."

"Shame," I tell her. "But we can always add that later. If they're anything like you, they're going to love to party."

"Party? What's a party?" she asks with a tired sigh as I pop open the can with a screwdriver and stir the paint with a stick. Lily disappears and comes back dressed in an old T-shirt and shorts. My eyes fix on her slender legs as she walks toward me. I get a flashback to them wrapping around me on my bed and I stand up straight, only to find myself an inch from her face. She holds my eyes for just long enough for the live wires to start sparkling up my forearms and over my chest, but I keep my expression in neutral till she looks away, shaking her head.

"What did I do?" I ask her, pouring paint into a tray.

"You know exactly what you *do*," she replies, stepping away from me to unwrap a brand-new roller. I honestly have no clue what she means, but before I can ask, her phone beeps and she grabs it up from the windowsill. I watch her eyebrows rise, then knit together, and I pick up another roller, ask her who's messaging her. Usually, I'm the one fielding calls that turn my face like this.

"It's Anthony," she tells me. "He's been texting me a bit. More than he used to. I think he wants to visit."

"The baby daddy?"

"If that's what you want to call him, yes." She says it as a question, like she's not sure of *who* he is to her, exactly. A flood of mixed emotions swoosh over my senses as she pushes a lock of hair behind her ear. I ask her when he started messaging her regularly and she tells me about a month ago. We stand side by side on the plastic sheeting, rolling color onto the walls. "Should I let him visit when they're born?" she asks me. "I know you weren't so keen before but…"

"It's not up to me," I tell her. This is not what I came here to talk about. I came here to finally discuss us…and this guy's intrusion irritates me more than it should. "I don't know, Carter, what does he want from you?"

"Why does he have to want anything?" she asks, and I sniff at the wall, rolling my brush over it too hard, sending paint splatters onto my shirt. Damn it.

"Well, does he want to support you going forward, or does he want one look at his creations before he disappears again forever into the sunset, on his bike?"

"He has every right to see them, I suppose," she says with a shrug. I put my brush down.

"He only has the rights you give him. You don't owe him anything, Lily. But I guess you have to ask yourself what *you* want."

She looks confused and sad for a second, and I know she feels conflicted. I lean the ladder against the wall and climb up. We paint in silence for a while before she stops and lowers herself to her knees on the floor.

"Grayson used to say I was too needy," she says quietly. I stop painting. A leaden ball has just formed in my stomach. She doesn't look up at me while she speaks. "He said a lot of things that stuck in my head and now I guess I overcompensate in some ways. I don't want to *need* anything or anyone, but I don't like cutting people off. It's not fair."

"I know you don't want to *need* anyone," I tell her softly. She's running her hands over her stomach and I step back down the ladder. This is the first time she's really said anything about what this guy did to her.

"I shouldn't have compared your situation with your mom to me and him," she says.

"It's okay."

"It's not okay. I don't know what you're dealing with exactly, Theo. I shouldn't have done that, it wasn't fair. Grayson was in a league of his own. He would reel me in, then shut me out. He'd tell me he loved me, then tell me I was a waste of space. I did everything I could to reach him, to make him realize he needed me. But I just came off like I was desperate and I ended up hating myself."

She pauses, and this time the tears really do come loose in her eyes. I lower myself to the floor beside her. We sit between the ladder and the paint cans, and Jasper looks on from the doorway, licking his paws. "How could I explain all this to *you*, without you thinking how stupid I was not to walk away sooner, Theo?"

"It's not easy to walk away. Trust me, I know," I tell her. "They get into our heads. There are good moments, when…" I swallow, I'm suddenly too hot. I've never said any of this out loud to anyone and it's making me more emotional than I want to be. "There are good moments when they love us, and it makes us think everything's gonna finally be all right."

"I used to cling to those moments so hard," she follows. "It only made the rejection worse. He wasn't always like that. I loved him for a long time. It's why I stayed…"

"I can imagine." I take her hand in mine and hold it tight. My heart beats a violent drum against my rib cage. She's been keeping all this inside her, and it's probably been eating away at her, too, the same as all this with Mom has been eating at me. "I know all about that," I say, turning my whole body to face her now. She turns my hand around in hers and looks at me sideways. The live wires spark again up my arms beneath the paint splatters.

"Listen, Lily, I owe you an apology," I begin. "I said I wouldn't hurt you, and I know my silence about all this has done that. I guess I also find it hard to talk about."

"Theo, you don't—"

"No, let me finish," I insist.

Jasper can probably tell my heart is hammering under my shirt, because he pads over and starts nuzzling me, before moving to Theo. Somewhat reluctantly, Theo pets his head while he talks about what's going on with his mother. I can't believe what I'm hearing.

He tells me how she refuses to take her meds, and how she refused to attend that appointment at Serenity Pines the day of my mat leave party, forcing him and Peonie to go on their own. He tells me how his whole childhood was a living hell, just waiting for her next flare-up, how he spent the whole time plotting the next escape in case he had to run, to protect his sister. He tells me that his mother got so mad at him once that she threw a kettle at his date, which broke so close to the woman's head that she blocked him at every angle soon after and refused to speak to him ever again.

He tells me how his father left without ever looking back. I can't even imagine the pain and damage that would have caused. The sense of abandonment. Theo is acting as mediator to this day. He's still looking after Pea, still concerned for his baby sister's welfare, and Pea's own family's, too. A new respect for him blooms around my heart, till I can hardly stand not touching him.

He rubs a hand across his chin and mouth, and I realize I've been staring at his lips since he started talking. "It's a mess, Carter."

"Your mess is part of you, and you've been

nothing but supportive of my own mess," I remind him, running my hands over my bump
softly. If I don't touch myself, I'll touch him.

His blue eyes lock with mine. There's a
warmth there, a gratitude that makes my heart
swell and forces a flock of giant butterflies to
buzz around inside me. For a second I feel myself leaning in ever so slightly. I'm drawn to
him like always, even more so now. I understand him, why he is the way he is, why he was
reluctant to tell me any of this before. He was
ashamed, like I was, for letting Grayson control me.

I catch myself, and I can't help a little laugh
escaping from my throat. He cocks his head and
asks me what could possibly be funny.

"The fact that you told me all that, and now I
understand—"

"You understand why I'm an emotionally
unavailable bachelor with a deep-rooted fear of
abandonment by the people who claim to love
me. Is that right?" Without warning, he picks up
the roller and flicks it at me lightly, sending an
arc of paint flying right at my face.

I shout out as speckles of sunset blush land on
my cheeks and neck and on my shirt. He looks at
me with a mischievous glint in his eye. It turns
me on more than it should, and I retaliate with
a swift flick of my own roller.

"Not fair!" He scrambles to his feet just as I do, and I raise the brush again.

"Okay, okay, truce!" he laughs, holding up his hands in surrender. Then he takes a step closer. My breath catches as he removes the roller from my hands. He drops it to the tray and faces me, and I watch his pulse throb at the base of his neck. Just his eyes on me now are undoing me. I am right back in his bedroom, hands against his hot skin, his muscles tightening under my fingers. We didn't kiss. We haven't kissed, ever, but I think I might die if I don't.

"Do you still think of me like that, Carter?" he asks. "Emotionally unavailable."

I falter a moment. My instinct is to tease him, tell him leopards don't change their spots. But he's here; he came to help me. He came to talk to me, and he's opened up more than I thought he ever would. "I care about you. A lot. I think you know that," he says.

My breath catches in my throat. It feels like my blood has turned into pancake syrup now. His eyes track mine and I can see the intensity of our conversation blowing like a storm in his gaze. He didn't have to tell me everything, the same as I had no intention of opening up about Grayson, but here we are. Something else just changed between us, an indelible line was drawn up between who we were and who we are. My pulse throbs at full throttle under my hot skin as I finally reach a hand to his face, trace a finger across his lips.

"I care about you, too," I admit, but there's an edge to my voice. I know he can see that protective shield around my heart. "It's complicated."

"Very," he agrees, leaning into my hand before catching it and holding it to his cheek. He closes his eyes, then brings my hand to his lips himself this time. My internal alarms are blaring, reminding me of all the reasons why this could be a disaster. He kisses my fingers and the action sends lightning bolts across my skin.

"Theo, we shouldn't," I whisper, though every fiber of my being screams otherwise. It's maddening, this pull toward him.

"We shouldn't," he agrees, his voice low, his breath mingling with mine. My body is short-circuiting; his eyes are electrifying my nerves. How does he do this? How do I let him? We're closer than ever, and I'm struggling to keep my resolve.

"This is *really* complicated."

"We've established that." The intensity in his gaze is almost too much, but I can't look away.

"I'm about to have twins, Theo."

He looks deep into my eyes. "I know that, Carter." He presses his forehead to mine, and I cast my gaze down to my bump between us.

His voice is a caress, soft and sincere, and I want to give in. I want to taste him. But this is only going to end badly; how can he not see that? He thinks he's changed, but has he? Will he feel this way when my babies arrive? I'll only start needing him, and then I'll be left for dust.

"Theo, I—"

Before I can protest, before I can even think of how to build up another wall, his lips find mine. Logic completely vanishes out the window. My arms wind around his neck as if they have a will of their own. The kiss isn't just a meeting of our mouths; it feels like the crashing together of everything we are—friends, confidants, colleagues, two people who have more in common than we ever knew before. It's so passionate, so all-consuming, that absolutely everything shrinks right down to the way his tongue dances over mine, and how his hands are sweeping along my back, up and down through my paint-splattered shirt, then tousling hungrily in my hair. I feel myself urging him closer, digging my nails into his skin, but there's only so close we can get with my bump between us. Still, we're totally lost in each other, breathless as our mouths grow more urgent, our teeth sinking into each other's lips softly, then releasing. Then...

"Ahem."

The sound jolts us apart. Reeling, I turn to see Rose standing in the doorway.

"I…um… I see I'm interrupting something," she says as I smooth down my shorts. Theo runs his hands through his hair and picks up the roller.

"Rose," I manage, heat flooding my cheeks. "We were just—"

"Painting," Theo finishes lamely, and he grimaces as he looks at me, which for some reason only makes me laugh. My heart is still thrashing wildly in my chest, and my legs still feel unstable. I lean against the wall as Rose studies us. Her lips twitch, and her knowing look informs me she's amused rather than disapproving, but I can't shake off the embarrassment.

"I thought you were out for the afternoon," I say, lamely.

"I forgot my book," she replies, holding up the textbook.

"Right, well, I should probably get back to it, too," I say quickly, gesturing toward the half-painted wall. Theo is painting again already, three rungs up the ladder.

"Of course, don't let me stop you." Rose backs out of the room, still smirking to herself, and I pretend not to see the pointed look she throws me as she leaves. I am going to hear about this later.

I turn to Theo, my heart still racing. "You should *not* have done that," I manage to whisper.

"Are you sure?" he shoots back at me. He waits for the front door to shut behind Rose and climbs back down the ladder.

"Yes," I tell him. I don't move an inch. My lips are still pulsing from our kiss. I want to tear his shirt off, roll in paint and command he makes love to me in the middle of the room, but…this is all so crazy. "I'm sure," I add, but the wobble in my voice betrays me.

I wait until he's inches from me, brushing loose strands of hair from my face. I have paint all over me, and so does he, and I know he knows I'm lying. The second I open my mouth to speak, a groan escapes instead and I pull him close again by the front of his shirt. In a heartbeat we're back in each other's arms, and in minutes our clothes are strewn around the room and all the inhibitions I thought I'd have, being the size of a bus and hornier than I've ever been in my life, seem to evaporate as we take it in turns to pleasure each other in ways I don't think I've even dared to envision with a man this ridiculously hot and into me. The only reason we don't have full sex is because it's so physically awkward, and I tell him I'd rather wait.

"Some things are worth waiting for," is his reply.

For the next month, we do this more than we probably should, falling into each other's arms as soon as we're alone, and sometimes even out in public. We go on actual dates to exhibitions, to parks and museums. He cooks me for after his shifts, rubs my feet. We talk a lot, about everything and nothing, and sometimes I can't imagine how we were only friends all this time, because I've never felt like I can be myself with anyone like this before, really, besides Rose. It's comfortable, but it's electric at the same time.

People stop to ask how "our" babies are doing, and every time I can't be bothered to explain, Theo puts on a straight face and tells them, "They're going to be TikTok influencers. It's all we've ever wanted for our children."

I don't think I've ever wanted to sleep with anyone as much as I want to sleep with Theo, but he doesn't push for it, and I tell myself as long as we don't do that, I won't fall in love. I'm getting pretty good at lying to myself, but I can't afford not to. I think I'm starting to need him, and I still can't stop the niggling feeling that with everything he has going round that head of his—with his mother, his sister, his work— that myself and my fast-approaching new role as a mother of twins will all prove too much for him eventually.

CHAPTER FOURTEEN

THE SUN IS a warm caress on my hatless head as Lily takes my arm and we watch another dog run for a ball along the Riverwalk. Finally, we're heading into spring. The skyscrapers glint in the sun, the river is sparkling and the tourists can't get enough selfie-stick photos of Chicago the way it was designed to be seen. An undeniably magnificent mile.

This is our fourth Sunday morning coffee walk in as many weeks. Seeing as Lily is almost thirty-six weeks into her pregnancy it's more like a waddle, then a sit-down, then another waddle, then another sit-down. It's at one of these sitting down points that Pea calls me. I'm seeing red by the time I hang up, but Lily is engrossed in something on her own phone now, so I hold in the fact that Delilah has reported her grandmother *sounded drunk this morning*. It was 10:00 a.m. when they spoke.

I fume in silence, watching the boats glide past on the water. It's too nice of a day to bring

Lily down. It's been a month or so of trying to reschedule things at Serenity Pines, and Mom still refuses to even entertain the notion of visiting, let alone staying there. We *can* force her. We can have them come collect her. But Pea is having second thoughts again, maybe because she's seen how happy I am these days.

I fix my eyes on another tourist boat that's drifting a little faster than the others toward the dock, but I'm pulled to Lily when she sighs at her phone. My jaw tightens instantly. She's messaging the motorcycling baby daddy, who suddenly seems to see himself as a candidate for Father of the Year. She looks at me sheepishly before sliding her phone back into her purse, and I stop myself from asking her what he wants. I know she hates it when she thinks I'm telling her what to do, and I know more about *why* she hates that now. Anyway, I'm more concerned about Mom being drunk at 10:00 a.m.

"You look displeased, Grasshopper," she observes, turning to face me properly.

"Sorry, there's trouble in the kingdom again, Princess," I reply, and she gives me that sympathetic frown that tells me I don't have to say any more. I kiss her, wrap my hand around hers on her lap. Right away, some of the tension floats from my back and shoulders and she smiles under my mouth.

"I thought you were still annoyed that I canceled on you for maternity yoga last night."

"Oh, I am," I tell her, scooping a hand behind her head and urging her closer. "But I used the time to dream up some other fun positions we can try."

"I'm looking forward to it," she tells me, but then she winces and presses a hand to her midsection and tells me the babies are kicking. When we resume our path along the waterfront I'm wary of every person coming toward her. If I could conjure a protective bubble around us, I would. I've never felt this way about anyone before in my life. Who'd have thought *not* having sex would make me more invested, more raw, more available? I guess she thinks I won't like making love to her like this, but I'm only concerned she'd be uncomfortable. I'm taking this thing one day at a time. Our emotional connection is so strong, it's like we make love with our minds sometimes. I can only imagine what the sex will be like in the future.

We've just rounded the corner when an almighty crash sends us staggering backward. My arm goes around her. Screams echo out ahead of us, followed by more anguished sounds and a lot of splashing. "What the—?"

I look at Lily, then we both start hurrying toward the dock. A small tour boat must have lost control, its engine sputtering before crashing into the Riverwalk with a sickening crunch. There's fiberglass everywhere, luggage floating in the water, and people floundering.

"We need to get them out!"

Lily looks stricken as she races for the edge with me, still clutching her bump. The impact has thrown the boat's passengers into the water like ragdolls and they're flailing about, grappling for fallen cases and swimming toward the sides.

"Help! Somebody help, I can't swim!" A scream pierces the air and I zero in on a young woman in the water, clutching the edge of the dock. I call for an ambulance quickly, tell Lily to assess the situation with the injured, and instruct a bystander to get some medical supplies from a nearby restaurant. I drop to my stomach at ground level and reach for the woman's hand. Her face is shock white and her eyes wide with terror as she grapples for my hand, just out of reach. Elsewhere, strangers are pulling others out of the ice-cold river, but just as I finally clasp this woman's fingers, she gasps and drops back in, and immediately she's floating out of my reach. I strip off my leather jacket and shoes, and I only just make out Lily calling my name before I dive into the water.

I reach the woman within seconds, turn her to her back and propel us back to the side with one arm. She's shivering, and so am I. This water is still freezing cold. "You're okay, ma'am. I've got you."

Two guys help haul her out and she drops to the deck, where someone drapes a towel over her shoulders and helps me back out with one hand. There's more chaos unfolding here than in the ER on the Fourth of July. A crowd is already taking photos, while others kneel to help the people on the ground.

"Theo, over here!" Lily's voice. I turn dripping wet to see her kneeling beside a man with a deep gash on his forehead, blood streaming down his face. She's already applying pressure with a scarf.

"Keep talking to him," I instruct, moving to assess the situation better. "Sir, can you hear me?"

"Y-yes," he stammers, wincing as Lily presses harder. I can see he's not okay.

"Good. You're all good," I tell him, anyway. Lily's brow is furrowed in concentration as she tears a gauze we've just been given. Even at nearly full term, she's a force to be reckoned with.

"His pulse is weak," she tells me, her voice strained. I can see she's struggling almost as much as this man; she's in no shape to be doing this but I know she would never forgive herself if she didn't. The cops are here now, ordering people this way, sending reporters and a TV crew in another. An ambulance is inching through. I can hear the sirens in the distance, too.

"Hang in there, Carter," I say, then I turn to a distraught young woman who's just been pulled from the water. "Ma'am, what's your name?"

"Angela," she gasps, shivering uncontrollably. "I can't find my cat!"

"Angela, do you have any injuries? Can you move everything?"

"Just cold...and my arm hurts," she whimpers, cradling her right arm protectively. "I need to find my cat...he's in a crate!"

"Okay, let me see." I snatch up the jacket I took off before and wrap it around her shoulders for warmth. "Lily, how's your guy doing?" I ask her as my eyes scan the dock and the water for a crate that might be holding a cat. I'm not even going to ask why there was a cat on a tourist boat...cat people are strange.

"Theo, he's losing consciousness!" Lily's voice sharpens, pulling me back to the man in her arms. He must have taken a big hit from the boat.

"Stay with us, buddy. Help is almost here," I coax as his eyes flutter. "What's your name?"

"A-Abdul," he rasps.

"Abdul, Doctor Carter here is good at this. Hang in there."

Lily has located more gauze and tape from the supplies going around the scene. Despite her cumbersome form, she works fast alongside me, wiping sweat from her brow. She's hot, and I'm freezing. I'm only just feeling how numbingly cold that water really was, when Angela's voice comes at me again over the wail of the sirens.

"Over there! My cat!" She and her friend are pointing over the side, beside themselves. They look like they're going to jump back in.

"Dammit," I mutter, glancing at Lily. "Can you handle things here?"

"Go," she urges, her eyes fierce. "I'll take care of them. Theo, be careful."

"You be careful," I warn, squeezing her hand before diving back into the chaos.

The icy water shocks my system all over again, but the adrenaline keeps me moving. The cat is alarmed and unsurprisingly feisty as I grab for the crate and drag it back with me. Angela takes it in floods of tears, sobbing, "Thank you, thank you, thank you!"

"Over here!" a man shouts now. How did we miss him before? He's trying to keep a child afloat, his son maybe. I thrash back through the water, grabbing the boy first.

"You're safe now. I've got you." I'm trying to reassure them but the cold water is seeping through my senses, slowing me down by the second. It's all I can do to haul his son to the side and lift him high into the waiting arms of a paramedic, but I have to go back for this guy. He's even colder, even weaker. Every muscle screams in protest, but I push through. I have to help everyone I can. On the dock, past the police car, the ambulance and the frenzied crowds, I see Lily, still on her knees, attending to someone else now. A middle-aged woman.

"We need more blankets," she yells as I haul my soaking body out of the water. "She's going into shock!"

I sprint back to Lily, dripping all over the boardwalk. I can't afford to think about how cold I am right now. I just wrap warm blankets around the shivering woman and help two paramedics load her onto a stretcher.

"Theo, you need to get warm," Lily tells me. I tell her I'm fine, that other people need them more than me.

"How are *you* holding up?" I ask her as I cast my eyes around the scene. I'm doing my best to regulate the pounding in my chest but I can hear it in my own voice.

"Pregnant, not helpless," she shoots back, before draping a blanket around me and holding me close. Her warmth seeps into me immediately. She pulls me harder into her, and for a brief moment as the cold air leaves my lungs and I press into her heat, I am completely, utterly, ir-revocably hers. It has been a long time since a woman I cared about cared about *me* this much.

"Move aside, please!" More paramedics swarm the scene, taking over the care of the people we've stabilized. One of them I know, and he looks between Lily and me in concern, asks if we're okay.

"We're okay," Lily breathes, finding my arm and guiding me to the side away from the crowds. Her hand lingers on her stomach for just a second too long. Any warmth she's just transitioned to my body chills over when her face crumples up.

I step closer. "Carter?"

"Yeah, just—" She winces again, clutching her belly. "Theo, something's wrong."

"What's happening?" I demand, cupping her elbow.

"Feels like…contractions," she gasps. Her face is paling now. I drop the blanket from my shoulders.

"Contractions? Are you sure?"

Now, of all the times that this could happen. It's too early.

She shoots me a look that's almost apologetic, right as she doubles over under another wave of pain.

"Not here, please, my loves," she wheezes

under her breath. "It's too early. There are too many people. This is not your moment."

"Maybe they weren't getting enough attention," I say, and I wrap an arm around her, start guiding her through the throng of onlookers. Journalists are already hovering, cameras flashing, microphones thrust forward.

"Miss, can you tell us what happened?" one reporter calls, her eyes zeroing in on Lily.

"Not now!" I snap, shielding Lily with my body. "She's in labor!" I flag down a paramedic, who rushes over with a stretcher. His eyes widen as he takes in Lily's condition.

"She's having contractions…she's thirty-six weeks," I explain urgently. "We need to get her to the hospital. Now."

He signals his team. They lift Lily onto the stretcher, securing her quickly.

"Theo?" Her eyes dart around the chaos for mine, and she reaches out for my hand. "Don't leave me."

"I'm here," I tell her, clasping her hand tightly. "I'm not going anywhere."

CHAPTER FIFTEEN

I DO MY best to breathe through the pain and panic, to focus on the squeak of the rubber-soled shoes against the sterile floor, the voices all around me in Evergreen's corridors. I can hear people talking about what's happened on the Riverwalk. Already there are photos online, apparently, of me and Theo. Theo saved a cat.

Focus on that, I tell myself, holding my belly as I draw deep breaths on my back and the familiar hospital walls rush past me.

"Contractions are five minutes apart, preterm labor," Theo barks at the nurse who's jogging alongside me. He's not holding my hand now. He's in full ER doctor mode, despite being soaking wet and no doubt freezing cold, and while I'm grateful there were paramedics already on the scene out there, this is even more complicated than I ever thought it would be. I should have been taken to Dawson's but there was no time, and with the city streets all clogged because of the accident at the dock, here I am.

Theo. I need him with me, whatever happens next. I don't want to do this alone.

As if reading my mind, Theo stops at the doors to room three. "You're in good hands, Lily. You know they'll look after you."

"No... Theo." Another contraction makes me flinch, then yell out as I'm rushed into the room, but Theo follows. He is tired, wet and visibly cold but he knows I need him.

"I'm not going anywhere," he tells me, and I nod and try to concentrate on my breathing. My babies are coming early. I can tell they're desperate to get out. Why did they choose today? Another contraction almost cripples me. I don't even know how long I lie here. I'm losing track of time now. It feels like hours pass. Sweat plasters my hair to my forehead. My throat feels raw from screaming, and the room is a blur of scrubs and surgical masks, and the sterile smell of antiseptic blending with my own fear. I'm told to push. I'm so weak. No one can prepare you for this.

"Doctor, heart rates are dropping," a nurse says.

I don't like her tone one bit but I trust her. I trust everyone here. Why did I want to go to Dawson's in the first place? I don't recognize the locum obstetrician but she knows who I am, like everyone here. Theo is at my side, and somehow

I manage to move my hand from my bulging belly and into his. I need his strength.

"Let's move quickly. We need those babies out now," the obstetrician warns. Her voice is steady but strained. "Lily, you need to focus. Push!"

"Come on, Lily," another nurse encourages, patting my leg gently.

"You're all good, Carter," Theo follows. I focus on his eyes. "You're almost there. You're doing so well, come on, make me proud."

Proud? He's proud of me? Tears stream down my face as my body struggles to comply with the things he and all these people are telling me to do. How exactly do I do this? I bear down with every ounce of strength I have left, feeling my body stretch and strain until I hear the words I've been dying to hear.

"Here comes Baby A."

A high-pitched cry fills the room. Relief washes over me.

"Baby A is just fine! Let's get ready, Baby B," Theo says, before anyone else has a chance.

His eyes are wet with tears and he's not even trying to hide them. Despite the pain ripping through me I am utterly lovestruck seeing the pride on his face. He looks like he might actually be their father; no one on the outside right now would have any reason to think otherwise. I can do this.

"You're almost there, Lily," he says, still squeezing my hand. "Keep going."

I can do this.

The glare of the overhead lights bears down on me as I pace the corridor. People who know me try to make conversation, try to congratulate me for being a hero on the dock, saving a cat as well as a kid; I can hardly believe it. And now this. My mind reels and spins with the magnitude of the day's events. I'm still cold and damp, and my hands are still trembling with the remnants of adrenaline. I shove them deep into my pockets. The muffled sounds of urgency seep through the closed doors of the delivery room and I want to go in there but I can't just yet. Rose is in there now, doting on her new niece and nephew.

I'm not leaving. Pea tries to call again, but this time I don't answer. I'm a wreck.

"Doctor Montgomery?" Eventually, a nurse's voice cuts through my thoughts. I'm told that I can see her again, and my heart lodges in my throat as I enter the room. There she is. Lily is pale, exhausted, but beaming, too. Rose is at her side. In Lily's arms, swaddled in the trademark hospital cotton, are her two tiny, perfect-looking babies. For once in my life, I can't seem to find any words. It almost feels like they're mine somehow, after knowing Lily the way I'm starting to know her. I'm connected by way of my connection to Lily.

I edge closer, and the air around us charges with something indefinable. My finger brushes against a tuft of dark hair that's so much like Lily's, and their smallness staggers me. A surge of protectiveness washes over me. It's so fierce it leaves me reeling. These babies, part of our story—they matter more than I can articulate. Rose shares the news with their dad, Geoff, on the phone, and I watch her watching me as she talks to him from across the room.

"Hey again," I say to the tiny boy and girl in Lily's arms. "Let's make it official. I'm Theo. You just couldn't wait to get here, huh?"

"Aren't they perfect?" Lily breathes out, her green eyes meeting mine.

"You did good, Carter. They *are* perfect," I tell her truthfully. We've already been told they're a little jaundiced, that due to the speedy birth and the distress they were in, it's best if they stay in the NICU for a while. It's nothing to worry about; Lily knows that. Rose knows that. She's still watching us together. I straighten up and my hand goes to swipe self-consciously at my jaw. I didn't realize how emotional I was till now. I had no idea how I'd feel in this moment. How is it possible that I feel so attached already?

"I'll leave you to rest," I tell Lily as the twins

are removed from her arms, ready to be moved to the NICU. I refrain from kissing her in front of everyone we know, even when she leans into me out of exhaustion, probably.

I've barely made it outside into the sunlight when Pea's name flashes up again on my phone. "Pea? Lily's fine, the babies are fine."

Pea was concerned about the boat incident and seeing me on the news. She has no idea that Lily has just given birth—why would she—and I'm forced to tell her what happened. I tell her the twins are fine but will have to spend a little while in the NICU, and Pea tells me it's not my fault. The second she does, is the second I wonder if it *is* my fault. I put Lily in danger again, letting her help, even though she wanted to. I put the twins into distress mode.

I can't shake the thought now. It strangles me as I walk toward the bus stop; we didn't take my car to the city and I rode in the ambulance here. I must look like a damp, disheveled disaster who's just dropped from the sky in a rainstorm, and I can't face the thought of talking to a cab driver.

On the bus, Delilah calls me. Pea said earlier that she went to a friend's house this morning. Maybe she also saw me on the news? Or TikTok, most likely. I call her back, and what she tells me almost makes me stop the bus. She's not at a friend's house; she's with my mother. Or rather, she's only just managed to escape.

"Escape what?"

"I'm telling you, Uncle Theo, because I don't want to upset Mom!"

I can barely believe what Delilah is telling me. She went over to her house, to give her one of her riding certificates, hoping her grandma would be proud of her and frame it. It escalated after Dee found a bottle of vodka in the laundry cupboard and tried to hide it. Mom caught her and it all blew up. After the argument to end all arguments, Mom locked her in the utility room for two hours. Dee's only just managed to escape through the window, relocate her phone and call me. This is bigger than any of us now.

When I'm home, I call Pea again. As predicted, she's upset. Very. I tell her we need to do something once and for all, no messing around, and absolutely no more taking no for an answer. Mom needs help if she's going to get better, if things in our *family* are really going to get better. I want to be there for Lily and the babies with all of me, with all of my attention. I owe them that. I need to at least *try* to get my life back.

They're so beautiful. I know I'm biased but they are. I trace the delicate outlines of my twins' faces, their tiny fists curling and uncurling in their amazing little dance of newborn reflexes. I've become obsessed with observing it already. My heart swells with a love so fierce it almost hurts every time I look into their soulful eyes. In the NICU's soft light I can pretend for a moment that everything is perfect.

"My loves," I murmur. "You're both so loved, you know that?"

My gaze flicks back to my phone, resting on the edge of an incubator. Still no messages from Theo. I've heard nothing for almost two entire days. When I call, it goes to his voice mail. The silence from him is deafening, especially after what happened on the dock. I don't even know if he's all right. Each passing second is a confirmation of my worst fears. I expected too much from him, practically forcing him to stay with me during the birth... I went too far, like I always do, and now, not only have I scared him off with my neediness and impending list of maternal responsibilities, our friendship is most probably in the toilet, too.

Rose appears in our private white room with fresh flowers. I force a smile to my face as she arranges them in the vase Dad brought in last night, and peers over the babies. I still can't quite believe that my own children are here in the neonatal unit. Despite Theo's noticeable absence,

I'm beyond grateful that I accidentally switched to Evergreen for their care.

"Have you decided on their names?" Rose asks quietly as her hand lands gently on my shoulder. My twin has been a steady anchor these past couple of days. She's reassured me I can do this on my own…well, with her help of course, but I still don't want to admit how much I need Theo. My gaze flits between the two sleeping forms.

"I thought I'd decided on Ollie and Winnie. But now they're here, I'm not so sure."

"Names are identities…destinies, almost," Rose says, and I arch my eyebrows at her. It's not like her to say stuff like this.

"Getting sentimental, are you?"

"It's my niece and nephew. Of course we have to give them the perfect names! Take your time, Lils. It'll come to you."

I nod and sigh, trying to channel peace as my mind goes to Theo again. For a few silly seconds you could have convinced me that he and I were… Ugh. The only thing we ever were was predictable, spontaneous, a disaster waiting to happen. He couldn't have run away any faster after the twins were born. I hate that I'm surprised, when I should be anything but.

I wish I could stop thinking about him. I reach out for my phone again, but the screen is dark and silent. I resist calling him, but I do quickly reply to the message from Anthony, aka *Miami Motorhead*. He wants to take a ride here from Miami on the bike, and he seems pretty serious about it. I figure what's the harm? I know I want nothing from him, or nothing to do with him, really, but I still don't think it's fair to deny him the right to see the twins if he wants to. I don't want them growing up and finding out I refused their birth father when he offered to come visit.

We're just discussing more potential baby names, like Amelia and Harley, maybe, when my phone rings and sends my heart catapulting up to my throat. But it's just an unknown number. The same number that has now called a few times. I decline it as usual.

"I take it that's not Theo?" Rose asks, scowling at the floor a second.

"Probably just someone selling new windows, or car insurance like last time," I tell her. No, thanks. I'm too tired for that. I have enough to deal with right now without pushy salesmen on my back. Theo is probably busy being a hero after the boating incident, soaking up the spotlight from female reporters and fans. He's probably finally figured out the magnitude of what this all involves for me, and for him, too, should he stay involved. Players will always play, and I've been well and truly played. If I wasn't so exhausted, I'd be furious at both him and myself.

Rose chews on her lip, fiddles with her glasses, then crosses her arms. I know this look.

"Maybe there's an explanation," she says. "But then again, maybe it's time to accept that Theo *isn't* going to be the rock you hoped for," she adds softly. "It's you and me, Lily. The twins have us, and we have each other—we are all we need, remember?"

"We are all we need," I echo, even as the sting of tears threatens to spill. I thought I knew him, or was starting to, at least. I thought I was different. I thought he promised to never hurt me.

"Hey." Rose nudges me. "First one to make the other laugh changes the diapers for a week when we're home."

"Deal," I reply. I love how she's here for me. She knows I'm devastated, but she's not about to let me dwell on it. She didn't want to ruin my fun with him while it lasted, but she knew, and I did, too, I guess, that Theo isn't built for anything long-term, no matter what he says or likes to think.

Rose doesn't say another word, but when my chin wobbles her arm comes up around me. It's all I can do not to cry into her arms, and it's pathetic. I am pathetic for thinking we could actually be something, but I bolted all doors shut against the possibility of another betrayal years ago, until Theo Montgomery, of all people, forced them back open.

"Men," Rose scoffs eventually into my hair. Her voice is laced with a bitterness I know stems from her deep-seated pain over what happened with David.

"Men," I mutter, brushing away a stray tear. The ache in my chest seems to deepen, till a cocktail of hormones and hurt makes it hard to breathe. The doctor on shift arrives to ask when we're leaving, and whether we need anything arranged, and I try to curb the hope in my voice as I ask her whether Theo has checked into his shifts in ER.

"Doctor Montgomery called in sick yesterday," she tells me, looking over my babies. "Haven't seen him since. He was quite the hero, diving into the river for those people, and the cat! Maybe he caught a cold."

"Maybe," I echo hollowly as Rose presses her lips together and looks away. I know she wants to comment but she knows she shouldn't; not here. We both know if Theo was really sick, he would at least be checking his phone. Has he actually taken time off work sick in order to avoid me? Anger courses through my bloodstream till I have to remind myself it doesn't matter. All that matters now is my babies, keeping them safe and protected. I am all they have.

Later, when Rose is helping me pack my bags, I send Theo a message, which he will no doubt see once he decides to acknowledge me. No point getting emotional, or questioning him or begging, not like I did with Grayson. I need to get out of this one with my dignity intact. I won't let him break me. I have two little people relying on me now and they need me to be strong.

Theo. Now that the twins are here I think it's best for me to take some time to get to know them by myself. I'll forever be grateful for our time together. See you when I'm back at work. Lily.

I'll let him off lightly if that is what he wants. Me, however? I will take my two tiny precious gifts from God home, where I will resume my new purpose, to make their lives as wonderful as possible, without Theo Montgomery or *any* man getting in our way.

CHAPTER SIXTEEN

THE YOUNG COURIER hands over the package that contains my new lifeline. "Sign here, please, Doctor Montgomery," he says, extending a small electronic pad toward me.

"Thanks," I mutter, scribbling my name with more force than necessary.

The moment he leaves, I tear into the paper and soon the phone buzzes to life. I insert the new SIM card connected to my old number, leave it all to update while I pour myself a glass of water and stare at Chicago through the windows. My old phone is somewhere on a rooftop belonging to one of my neighbors, along with Pea's. If I knew Mom was going to toss them out there, I'd have locked them away before she got here, but at least *she* is safe now, and so is Delilah and so are we. She won't be leaving Serenity Pines for a while, and hopefully by the time she does, she won't still be out to throttle me.

The past few days have been hell. The confrontation with my mother was more like a detonation of years of pent-up frustration on my part, and denial on hers.

"Theo Montgomery!" Mom spat my name out like it was poison. For a moment I truly thought she was about to throw the kettle at me. "I am *not* going to rot in some institution!"

"Mom, it's specialized hospitalization, in a nice place. It's more like a retreat—" I tried to reason with her. She was the Elizabeth Montgomery I remember from my childhood, the one I would have done anything to protect Pea from, and she was not about to be reasoned with.

"I am your mother! Don't you care about me at all? How can you lock me away like an animal?"

I told her she won't be locked away, that she'll be cared for by the best team north of Chicago. She didn't know then that there were people due to arrive at my place any second, or that Pea had lured her here for collection, where she wouldn't be able to make a scene in public.

"You think because you play doctor all day, you can diagnose me?"

"Enough, Mother, I've had enough!"

Pea's voice shocked us all, even her. It was nothing like I've ever heard from my sister.

"Theo has only ever tried to help you, and me. He is a good brother and son. Either you accept our help, or I'm done, and you'll never see your granddaughter again."

I have to admit I was impressed. It was a standoff after that, like the Wild West minus the pistols. I moved the kettle. Mom snatched up my phone instead. She had the audacity to look me in the eyes as she tossed it right out the window. She managed to get Pea's next and awarded it the same fate.

"Try and get them to collect me now!"

She had no idea that the long-suffering Pablo had already agreed to help us, and was waiting outside to bring the people from Serenity Pines upstairs. We tried our best not to react in anger about the phones; it would have only made it worse. And then, the dam broke. Mom's shoulders slumped and I watched the fight drain out of her like air from a punctured tire. We argued for a while, until finally, she relented. She was no doubt fueled by the thought of never seeing Delilah again.

The aftermath is a blur—slammed doors, hushed conversations in a locked van, more tears, a whirlwind trip to Serenity Pines the next day to see her in her new pine-scented Lake Forest home away from home. Pea felt wretched. Her big heart is totally broken by what she's had to do. I've spent the past two nights with her and her husband, and Delilah; no phones, just each other. I've barely come up for air until now, and I'm sure Lily and I have a lot to catch up on. I tried to call her from the Serenity Pines landline a few times, but she didn't pick up. I could've left a message but I was all up in my head with a thousand things to say and in the end, it was better not to bother her with my issues. She's got her hands full, I'm sure. I'll talk to her when the twins are home.

Finally, my new phone has updated. My heart is a riot. The world narrows down to the glow of the screen as I read the last one from Carter.

Now that the twins are here I think it's best for me to take some time to get to know them by myself...

Wait. What?

I read it again, then again. She cannot be serious. I stare at my phone like it might ping more answers at me but it doesn't. She sent this yesterday. I call her instantly. The phone rings out, so I try again and finally she answers.

"Theo—" She sounds surprised. Behind her I can hear gurgling and laughing, and the sound of a guy talking to Rose, I think. She lowers her voice, hisses at me. "Theo, where have you been?"

"It's a long story, Carter, but I just saw your message. Are you serious? You want more space from me *now*?"

She's silent for a long while. I hear her walking to another room, closing a door behind her. "Who's there with you? Are you at home?" I ask. I don't know why but my instincts are primed for some kind of reply I'm not ready to hear. None of this adds up.

"You weren't here," she says slowly. She almost sounds confused before she sighs heavily. "You never even *called* me."

"I tried to," I protest but she cuts me off.

"Theo, I meant what I said, okay? I just need some time with the twins, to get to know them. And you clearly have a lot going on. You don't need me, or this."

I refuse to hear this. I have to swallow hard to keep my tone in check. "Lily, something's happened. What's going on?"

"Theo, we both know this was never going to be anything more than two friends messing around. I have to get serious. I'm a mother now."

"Stop it, Carter," I tell her. Abandonment and rejection don't just sting; they burn. My fists clench as I walk back to the kitchen. I tell her I can explain everything, but she cuts me off, distracted.

"I have to go, Theo. Take care, okay?"

The call ends and I stand rooted to the floor. *Take care?*

I scroll through the log of missed calls and

messages. She called me a couple times before sending that message. Maybe she did want to talk it through in person…or maybe she *was* just waiting to yank the bandage off and end it over the phone. Either way, I spent my whole life backing off, letting other people who claim to care about me dictate my fate. I'm not letting Carter off this easy.

The traffic on Maple Avenue is a slow-moving serpent. I drum my fingers on the steering wheel. There's a gnawing restlessness in my chest that I've never felt before over a woman. I hate it, but I love her. It crept up on me but it's true. The sight of the slow-down sign flashes a memory at me—Lily, laughing, crouching behind my car in the snow, her pregnant self behind the banner while I kept watch. That feels like ages ago already. I loved her then, too. Maybe I always have. How did this go wrong? Maybe she does still secretly blame me for the twins being born into all that drama and stress, for putting them at risk?

I park on the street outside her house. There's a shiny red Indian Chief Vintage parked outside and all right…it's a *nice* bike. I can tell it's seen some miles. I grab up the fresh flowers and the stuffed giraffe and antelope I bought her weeks ago in secret at the zoo, and step onto the street.

I'm actually admiring the bike up close when a shadow in her front window makes me pause. There's a stranger in the house, a man cradling one of the twins. He looks so effortlessly dad-like with the baby that my heart stutters some-where around my throat, then sinks. He lifts the baby high, mouthing a coo of affection and… I know who it is. The bike belongs to him. How did I not put two and two together before now? He must have ridden all the way here on it from Florida. This was who I heard laughing with Rose just now over the phone.

Something inside me shatters. Maybe every-thing. I can't go in there now.

I drop the gifts back to the empty seat. My hands clench the steering wheel until my knuck-les turn whiter than white. Lily has been un-reachable and now…well, it's pretty obvious why. She's been wanting to ask this guy here for months, I've seen her on the phone to him! How could I have been so sure of "us," as to think she wouldn't want to at least give things a go with the actual father of her babies, especially after what I did, or didn't do at the dock? After I kept everything about Mom from her for so long.

I should drive away, but I can't seem to look away from the window. He's tall with a mop of curly, thick hair that screams bohemian artist—someone who can simply hop on his bike and be anywhere, whenever he chooses. But somehow, he still couldn't be *here* till now. And she's choosing *him*! It feels like a punch to the gut. I'm swallowing back more betrayal and hurt than I can even try and fathom, watching him cavort around the living room like he belongs here. I want to storm in and demand answers.

Think, Montgomery. Flying off the handle won't help anyone.

What right do I have, anyway? Lily is a free agent. She can invite anyone she damn well pleases into her home, into her life. It's just that the panic clawing at my chest is way too much like the feeling I knew as a kid, knowing my dad was gone, knowing Mom wanted *me* gone, too. There's no way I'm letting that agony consume me again.

With a last searing look at the window, I put the car in Reverse and drive away. To think I was going to ask Lily Carter to be my girl, officially. I was actually going to admit to her face that I've fallen so deeply in love with her that I've started wishing with all my stupid heart that I could raise those kids with her, together.

CHAPTER SEVENTEEN

"AMELIA, NO, NO, NO..."

My voice cracks as I stare at my baby girl in the crib. Her tiny chest is heaving and her forehead is burning up. I quickly check Harley. He seems fine, sleeping like a log, but Amelia...

Fear scratches like nails at my throat as I swallow it back and tell myself to breathe. Just moments ago I was humming a lullaby to Jasper in the kitchen, and now, now something is really wrong. I tear open my medical bag. Two months into caring for the twins at home, I'd just been getting used to not needing it.

The thermometer beeps, and the numbers scream danger: one hundred and four degrees. Febrile seizure territory. Rose isn't home; she's off at some conference, and this is the first time I've been left alone since they were born, since I booted Theo out of our lives and Anthony rode off on his bike. I force myself to calm down. This is what I do; this is what I have to handle...

Theo. He's probably at the hospital. All I can think is *I need Theo.*

"All right, Amelia, Mommy's got you." I wrap her in a cool towel, pushing past the terror. As her little body shudders, Theo's steady hands flash into my mind again. This is not the time to be dwelling on the way he used to hold me, but I need him. I need him *now.*

I bundle up the sleeping pair and somehow fix the car seats in place. Jasper looks at me startled, and I tell him to guard the house while we're out. The drive is a blur of stoplights and honking horns, but my focus stays laser-sharp on the rearview mirror, where Amelia's car seat is strapped in tight. At every red light, I twist around to check if she's still breathing. "You're going to be fine, baby girl."

The familiar sterile smell hits me as I burst through the doors. "Help, emergency! I need help here, please!"

Despite this being the place that molded my professional status, I don't even know who I am right now. All I can think of is my baby. Again, I tell myself to maintain even a small glimmer of calm but I must look like a crazy person, holding one child and swinging around with another strapped to my chest. Heads turn, and then he's here—Theo, his blue scrubs clinging to him like superhero garb under his white coat, his blue eyes locking on to mine. Thank God. I almost fling myself onto him, but somehow I manage not to.

"Theo, it's Amelia. She's—"

"Exam room four, now," he cuts in, taking charge as he runs for a gurney.

He barely looks at me, but still, somehow he's all I need to feel safer, calmer. I follow him as they take over. Awkwardness hangs between us, thick and tangible after so long apart, I can feel it, even if he can't, but this is about Amelia.

"Talk to me, Carter," he says as we hurry alongside the gurney. Nurse Amber offers to take Harley off my hands. Gratefully, I accept and untie him from my chest but it does nothing to regulate my breathing.

"High fever, sudden onset. I'm worried it's meningitis…or…" My words trail off and I struggle to maintain my calm.

"Okay, let's get her stabilized," he says, and when his hand brushes against mine, a jolt of familiarity pierces through the chaos. We haven't touched in months, but his presence is still as grounding as it came to be before…well, before I told him and myself I didn't need him. I pushed him away, I know I did, and I've been agonizing over it ever since, along with dirty diapers and screaming in the middle of the night and accepting that I only have time to shower every two days. But it was the right thing to do; I didn't want to need him, only for him to pull away from me *and* my babies yet again.

We're in room four now. "Doctor Montgomery, she's seizing!"

Someone holds me back and ushers me to the corner of the room. I feel like I'm stuck in a bad dream.

"Get me two mgs of lorazepam, stat!" Theo barks.

The monitor beeps erratically, and I've no doubt my heartbeat is the same. I can help, I know I can. Theo knows I can, and this is my baby! But he doesn't let me close and neither does anyone else, of course. It's all I can do not to be thrown from the room as he starts an IV line.

"Come on, baby girl, stay with us," I hear him say. "I need a CBC, blood culture and lumbar puncture on deck. Temperature's spiked."

Everything becomes a blur around me as my gaze flicks between my baby and Theo's face. This is not exactly how I pictured a reunion. I don't deserve one at all, probably.

"Seizure's subsiding," he declares suddenly. His shoulders lose some of their stiffness as the meds take effect in front of us. Amelia's little chest is rising and falling more evenly now and finally, I can breathe a little more normally myself, even as the tests are done and I walk with them to the neonatal. He doesn't speak to me, and I don't speak to him. Why would he speak to me at this point? He's doing his job, but he must think I'm awful. I was angry and insecure when I sent that initial message, and then, when he called me I had Anthony in the house, I was distracted and in shock. I've been so selfish. I did to him the one thing he must hate most in order to save face. I was the one who served him his worst fear on a plate. I cut him out, made him feel like he didn't matter. But then, he didn't try to reach me. He didn't try at all. I haven't heard from him.

With a few colleagues surrounding us now, I don't miss how their eyes flit between us, like they're sure something is about to happen. My chin is doing a strange dance as I will it not to wobble. I'm just so exhausted. It feels like forever passes by as I wait for the tests that prove she's in the clear, drumming my already bitten nails to the chair in the private room Amber ushers me into, along with a vat of tea that I can barely touch. She's fine, it was just a febrile convulsion. I should feel a bit silly really but all I feel is even more exhausted and close to tears. I'm about to leave the room when Theo appears, and sees I'm alone.

He steps in and shuts the door behind him, pulling off his gloves.

"You saved her life, Theo," I choke. Finally, I can let all these crazy emotions free and it's more like an avalanche as he steps toward me, jaw clenched. His breath ruffles my hair and my nerve endings tingle as he leans into me.

"I would rather die than let anything happen to them, or you. Don't you know that?"

All the breath leaves my body. The second he looks away, his eyes glaze over with something like despair and it almost breaks me completely.

"Theo, I'm so sorry," I manage. I'm standing here in front of him, a few rooms down from the bathroom where I first found out I was pregnant, and I'm falling into more pieces than I did then. His arms come up around me, awkwardly at first, then tighter, till the four pens in his pocket are digging into my breast. I don't even care.

"It's okay, Carter," he whispers. He sighs against my hair, and his hand comes up to cradle the back of my head. "She'll be okay, I promise, don't worry."

The gesture, the familiar warmth of him, and the promise in his voice make me want to kiss him right here, pressed up against the cold porcelain sink, but I don't. I just fall back into his eyes. "I thought I was going to lose her... I couldn't handle it," I admit. "Not on top of losing you."

"I've been here the whole time, Carter," he says. "You just…you made your choice."

"My choice?" I try to stay afloat in his eyes, where everything used to make sense. But the world feels like it's spinning out of my control again. Outside I can hear Harley's guttural howl. Amber is still with him while I gather myself back together, but he needs feeding. I need to get back to my duties. I don't want to need this man in front of me, but I do. I don't want to risk more rejection but I also can't continue doing all of this without him, even if we just go back to being friends.

"Can we talk later?" I say, one hand on the door now. I feel so helpless. Harley is still screaming. I'm a terrible mother, but I love this man, and I can't just let this go.

He lowers his eyes, and my heart breaks as he shakes his head. Then, he sighs long and hard, so hard I feel the fabric of my shirt move around my collarbone. "Let me know when it's a good time to come over," he says.

I knew I still wanted her as more than a friend the second I saw her in the hospital with Amelia. I know it even more now that her door's swinging open and she's standing barefoot in front of me. I don't know what I'm doing exactly. Lily is with someone else, which maybe went into my decision not to buy her flowers this time, but I agreed to talk and she agreed to have me over, so here we are. I guess if we can salvage a friendship I'll have to be all right with it but seeing her now just makes me realize how much I've missed being more than her friend.

"Theo...you're early."

"Believe it or not, the traffic was fine, and no one had to hold me up by stopping to pee."

"Well, that's a good thing, seeing as you hung the banner up over your bed," she says dryly, but the smirk on her pretty mouth makes my heart speed up.

"I come bearing gifts," I tell her, lifting the stuffed toys for her to see, and she motions me past her into the house.

She's wearing a plain white shirt, tucked into denim shorts. Maybe I got used to seeing her bump, but her slender frame is kind of strange now. She almost looks the same as she did before the pregnancy; slim, petite, with legs like a damn gazelle. Her hair's all loose and longer now, and I like how it falls around her shoulders as she leads us to the living room.

"Motherhood suits you, Carter," I say before I can stop myself. She looks at me and a soft blush creeps up her neck and onto her cheeks. "I'm serious, you look good."

"Thank you," she replies, looking away quickly.

I'm nervous as hell right now and I don't even know why. I know I messed things up, not following up after I saw her with that guy. I couldn't even bring myself to send a message; she made her choice. She didn't message me, either.

There's a double crib in the living room, I assume, so she won't have to keep the twins in the nursery all the time. My breath hitches as I catch sight of them snoozing peacefully.

"Harley and Amelia," I murmur, stepping closer. They're so perfect. I send a silent prayer to whoever's listening that Amelia is good as new after that scare. The tiny girl stirs. Her little fist punches the air before her arms reach up as if she recognizes me. Does she? Lily lets out a huff of surprise, like she's wondering the same thing. I know it's impossible, but awe turns into annoyance at myself as I watch the baby's face scrunch and un-scrunch. I've missed two months already.

Lily picks up Amelia and asks if I want to hold her. I'm not sure if I do. I'll only get attached. But Lily places her into my arms and her little mouth puckers, and her big eyes stare up at me, and I'm attached again, just like that. Great.

"Harley usually sleeps like a log. But Amelia... Rose says she's got a sense of people," Lily says as she crosses to the open kitchen to make some tea. Her voice is tinged with pride and tenderness, and a thousand layers of maternal love I never got to witness as a kid myself, and I know why I'm here. I want to be a part of this, whatever that means. Even if Carter's with…him.

"So, did you name Harley after the bike?" I ask, placing Amelia back in the cot. Her hair is the cutest tuft of dark brown. Her skin, soft as silk and warm, gives off a scent you could only describe as baby. I hope this motorcycle man is good to them both. I hope he appreciates what he's got because her last guy didn't and neither did I, for a long time.

"Why would I do that?" Lily's hands are steady as she passes me the cup, but I can see the flutter in her eyelids, the way her gaze darts away just before our fingers brush. I open my mouth to explain, but stop myself. An ocean of unsaid words seems to stretch out as she sits at the other end of the couch.

She picks up the blue giraffe I brought, along with the cute red antelope. "I don't know why I expected a grasshopper," she says. I can hear the nerves in her voice as she turns it over in her hands. I sit back in the couch.

"Well, I did bring flowers for you, too, last time…but they're dead now. Obviously."

"Flowers?" Confusion laces her voice. Her brows knit together. "Last time?"

"Yeah, I drove here, after we spoke on the

phone," I confess. "I wanted to talk and explain what happened with Mom, why you didn't hear from me for two days after they were born. But I never made it to the door."

I watch the realization dawn on her face. "Theo, I had no idea."

"How would you?"

She lowers her head; she's embarrassed I saw them, I bet. "I'm sorry," she says eventually. "The message I sent you... I didn't mean... I know it must have hurt after everything you've been going through with your mom."

"It's all right." I cut her off before she can spiral into an apology that neither of us needs right now. It's easier to play the part of the rational one than to admit how much seeing that guy here stung that day. "I should've known you'd need someone with more to offer. Like the babies' father."

The words still feel like lead on my tongue. "How's it going, anyway? The long-distance thing between here and Miami?"

I casually mention seeing the motorcycle outside last time, and seeing him through the window with the twins. I brace myself for her response. I have to be ready to hear about the life she's building without me in it. But she's looking at me like I've grown a second head.

"Theo, he's not involved at all! He came by

once after they were born, offered to set aside money for their college fund each month, in case they need it later, but that's it. We agreed I wouldn't get any other help from him—it was my choice to keep them after all. My decision to do this alone. Besides, he's seeing someone."

I'm listening to all this from some place outside myself, processing what she's telling me. All these little pieces of a puzzle that have been floating around in my skull since that day, they're coming together. I shift closer to her on the couch.

"He only came by the one time?" I ask her. I need this clarified. I need to understand if what I'm hearing is true.

"I know you don't like that I let him, but he had every right to see them. I make my own rules, Theo."

"Of course you do," I tell her.

"He must have come by at the same time you did." She taps her fingers to the cushion between us like they're looking for somewhere to go. I take her hand and draw it to my lap and she shifts even closer.

"This is my fault," she says, meeting my eyes. "I was trying to give you a chance to get out of what we started before you could do the same to me. I compared you to…him…and what he would have done, and that wasn't fair."

"Well, maybe I should have fought harder for us, whatever it was I thought I saw with you and Anthony. I was just overwhelmed, I guess. There was a lot going on."

"I hurt you," Lily says, and she presses a hand to my face. "I shut you out, Theo, and I'm so sorry."

I want to tell her it doesn't matter, but we both know it does, that we're both sorry for getting the present all tangled up in the past. I tell her exactly what happened with Mom and Serenity Pines, and how Pea has really come into her own since Mom was forced to finally get treatment. She's excelling at work, and I don't have to dread seeing her name flash up on my phone anymore. We both know things can't ever get that bad again, but Mom is slowly returning to a slightly more manageable and tolerable version of herself under supervision, and hasn't attempted to use any kitchenware as weapons, which is a very good sign.

Lily tells me all about the struggles of single parenthood, but also how it's the most rewarding thing she's ever done all by herself. When we lay all these issues bare between us like open wounds, I just want her more. Somehow, throughout our conversation, we've closed any remaining space left between us and she's pressed up against me now, her leg to mine, my hands in hers.

Our words run dry until we're just sitting here, and she's looking into my eyes like she wants me to kiss her.

"I think I love you. Tell me I've finally lost my mind," she says eventually.

My heart lurches upward so hard it almost leaves my mouth, but I manage a laugh as I lean in to her. "If you've lost your mind then so have I, because I'm pretty sure I'm in love with you, too, Carter."

She moans softly into my shoulder a moment. "Theo…"

"And I still want to be here for you and the twins." My gaze flickers to the sleeping twins, then back to her. "If you'll let me."

"I think you mean if *Rose* still lets you," she says with a smile, but she's pressing her forehead to mine and inching a kiss down my nose. When our lips meet, the world tunnels into the softness of her mouth, the surrender of her body against mine. I can tell she's not going to let anyone come between us, but I will prove to anyone who needs it that I'm worthy of this woman and these kids. I want all of it, the mess, the chaos, the midnight diaper changes. Maybe a kid of our own; it's crossed my mind. I want to continue rebuilding my family with a solid foundation of love, and yes, that includes my mother. I also want to keep on adding to it, so no one has to *ever* think they're alone.

Lily pulls away slightly, studies my eyes. "There's one thing I need from you, if we're really going to make this work."

I frown at her. "No, I will not remove that banner from my ceiling. I want you to look at it every time I make love to you and remember how we started."

She grabs fistfuls of my hair, and I pull her astride me as she laughs. We both know there's no banner on my ceiling but I'm never going to let her forget that day. "That's not how we started, Theo," she says.

I remind her that that was the day I started falling in love with her, because looking back I think it's probably true. I tell her when I saw her at the fundraiser, challenging that doctor, then helping a man through and out the other side of a heart attack…what could possibly be hotter than that? For some reason, it only makes her kiss me harder. It's only when the cat pads in and attempts to curl round my legs that she remembers.

"Jasper was here first," she tells me. "And he and his fur are not going anywhere." She holds my hands above my head now and clenches her thighs around me. "I need to hear you say it. Jasper is King."

"Jasper is King, my princess," I tell her without missing a beat.

I don't mean it at all, but when she kisses me like this, I'll say anything. Besides, I'll probably even wind up *liking* the cat eventually, because I plan on being here a whole lot more from now on.

Almost a year later

Theo walks into the room. I stop with my stitching. It's proving beyond my current skill set to attach the newest patch onto the quilt that's taking up the entire dining table. He checks the cake he's baking in the oven, which already smells amazing, then he leans against the wall, playing with the string of a balloon that's floated up to the ceiling.

"You'll still be trying to stitch that when you're a hundred years old at this rate," he says, and when he sees I'm looking, he bends down to pet Jasper and makes a thing of *not* pulling a face and *not* rubbing his furry hands on his shirt after. "I could have learned to build an airplane faster."

"Why don't you learn to build airplanes, then?" I tell him. "You really don't have any recognizable skills, you know, except for the boxing and the doctor stuff—"

"Doctor *stuff*?"

I laugh as he puts his arms around me from behind and kisses the side of my neck about six times in a row. Then he whispers in my ear: "I think I've proven my many skills to you at this point, but please, let me know if you need me to trial any more with you."

I push my chair back and put my arms around him fully, and he lifts me onto the kitchen counter, standing between my legs. We kiss while we're laughing but soon, as it often does, our laughter morphs into something not entirely suitable for a kitchen that's expecting guests any second.

I push him off as Rose's footsteps sound out in the hall. Theo smacks my backside on the way back to the nursery where the twins are napping, and I pick up my stitching as the blush paints my cheeks. How is today their first birthday already? How has it been a whole year since their arrival, and almost a year since Theo and I decided to give things a shot, as more than friends?

Rose looks exasperated as she finds me. She's wearing a blue tailored blazer and smart suit pants and she throws her purse on the couch and flops down beside it. She's only just gotten home from her breakfast coffee date with a guy she met on a dating app, at Theo's encouragement of course. He loves to tell her that anyone who looks like *me* can totally score the second best-looking, second most successful man in Chicago.

"I give up. That was a complete waste of a morning," she declares, covering her eyes with her palms and groaning.

"Another bad date?" Theo ventures, coming back into the room with a spare balloon that floated outside to the hall.

"It was disastrous. He thought it would be *fun* to bring his pet snake to the diner. A snake, guys! He said he had an appointment at the vet after meeting me…two birds one stone kinda thing."

"Okay, no, that's not normal." Theo frowns. "Was it wrapped around his neck like a scarf?"

I set aside my sewing as they discuss the pitfalls of dating people with pets, and again Theo makes a thing of reminding me how much he loves Jasper now. Then Rose pulls a small green envelope from her purse.

"I forgot. I prepared something else for the time capsule when snake guy left."

Theo perks up, intrigued. The time capsule was his idea. We've been adding stuff to it for months with the idea being that we'll bury it today and open it when the twins turn eigh-

teen. Part of me was reluctant at first, because…
well…does Theo really anticipate being here
with me to open it eighteen years from now?
I know that's my old issues struggling for attention, though. Sometimes they try to surface
when I least expect it, but he hasn't gone anywhere, and instead we've kind of built a comfortable routine around him visiting me here, and me
visiting him at his place. Sometimes I take the
twins. Sometimes I leave them with the nanny,
or my dad. I hate to admit it but those are my favorite times, not because I don't enjoy the twins
being around, but adults need alone time. And
Theo's bedroom is my absolute favorite place
for us to be alone. He was lying about the banner on the ceiling, obviously, but when I'm with
him I wouldn't notice anything, anyway, even if
a million spiders were up there spinning webs
and watching us.

"It's a letter," Rose explains, putting it down
between us. "I wrote to them about everything
that's happened to their favorite aunt this year.
Figured it would be nice to have something personal from Madame Spinster Rose to read when
they're older."

"Oh, stop it," I tell her. Rose wants kids of her
own, which of course has to start with her getting back on the scene. I don't want her to give
up. I want her to find a love like Theo and I have

found, as impossible as it once seemed for either of us. But she doesn't believe it could ever happen. She says we are one in a million. I say she's crazy…we are four in a million, because we wouldn't be so in love if Amelia and Harley hadn't come into the world.

"Eighteen years will go so fast," I say. I can already picture them as teenagers. It really doesn't seem that long ago that I was eighteen myself. If I'd known what I'd have to endure to get to this point, would I have done anything differently? Sometimes I wonder. If I hadn't gone through all that, I wouldn't be with Theo now. We wouldn't have smashed all our stupid walls down to uncover the absolute best in each other.

"Do we want chocolate icing, or vanilla?" Theo's heading to the kitchen counter. He's obsessed with making cakes now.

"Both," I tell him.

"And raspberries," Rose adds.

"Your wish is my command, ladies."

Rose disappears to change for the twins' party. I smile as I keep on sewing, and Theo whips up icing in comfortable silence while I sneak looks at his backside and remind myself not to pinch it when our family is here. Delilah loves us together, but she has her limits.

There was a time when all of this would have scared me, when accepting Theo's love also meant living in fear that he might leave me. I guess he felt the same way for a long time, and somehow, through constant open communication and honesty…and amazing sex…honestly, it's the best…we've found what we really need in each other. Everyone at work has been so supportive of our relationship, too, since I started back at the NICU.

The doorbell chimes. I guess the party has started. I stand up, but Theo catches me, pressing a chocolatey kiss to my mouth that makes me swoon. "Is it wrong that I want them to leave already?" he whispers against my lips, right before grabbing my backside and urging my hip bones hard into him. I tell him no, not at all. He flashes that mischievous look that sends shivers down my spine. And then…

Peonie and Delilah step in from the hallway, arms laden with brightly wrapped gifts.

"Where are they?" Peonie exclaims, her voice ringing with excitement as she hands me a soft, squishy gift-wrapped parcel. "Where are my beauties?"

"Napping, they'll join us later. Peonie, these are…" I trail off as I unwrap the parcel and pull out two tiny onesies, and Theo gets up to take the cake out of the oven.

Delilah smiles softly. "Grandma made them," she announces.

They all look so proud all of a sudden, and peaceful. I sigh, holding them up. "They're gorgeous…we'll dress them in these when we visit next."

Theo goes a little quiet, pouring on the icing while we chat around the table, but it's only when he puts the cake down in front of us that I realize something is going on. He looks…not like himself.

"Okay," he starts. "Before we devour my latest creation, and while we're in a celebratory mood…"

Everyone at the table quietens down. I feel my own heart miss a beat or three, as every pair of eyes lands on me. "Theo, what are you—?"

My breath hitches as he drops down onto one knee. A small velvet box has somehow materialized in his hand. The room seems to shrink until it's just us.

"Lily Carter," he begins, and even though I know him to be the master of emergencies, his voice wavers and he's vulnerable and raw, the man I fell in love with a hundred times over. "I've been your wingman through double shifts, diaper disasters, roadside emergencies and pretty much everything in between for almost a year and that is long enough for me…"

He trails off as my hand lands softly over my mouth.

"It's long enough for me to know that I am yours, and you are mine and we belong together, Carter. Will you take me off the market forever? Will you do me the greatest honor imaginable and marry me?" He leans in, so only I can hear. "I promise, it will be your one and only wedding, and it *will* be spectacular."

I can barely breathe. Rose is squealing suddenly. So is Peonie, but luckily, from the way she's slapping him on the back, she's still ecstatic. Tears blur my vision, but his blue eyes are imploring through the haze, waiting for my response. My hands tremble, reaching for his.

"Yes, Grasshopper. Yes, I will do you that honor."

Delilah pulls a face. "Grasshopper? What?"

Theo ignores her. "Good, because I don't think I could return the ring at this point," he says. Then he winks at me. "It was *very* expensive."

He takes my hand and slips the diamond onto my finger. I gasp, tell him it's gorgeous, which it is, no joke. How on earth did he keep this a secret? How long has he been planning this?

Then, as if on cue, an indignant wail pierces our celebratory bubble, followed by another. The twins are perfectly synchronized as usual.

"I can hear they're critiquing my proposal," Theo announces, standing swiftly, taking me with him. "Let's go appease our pint-size crit-ics, will we, future wife?"

The cries dissipate as soon as we enter the nursery. Theo cradles Amelia and I hold Har-ley, admiring my ring the whole time we change them. He just proposed. Theo Montgomery will be my husband! What will everyone at Ever-green say on Monday?

"Ready to go back in there?" Theo's question pulls me back to the present, and to our family, waiting in the kitchen.

"In a minute," I whisper, leaning into him. I think I need another minute.

His lips find mine and he kisses me in a way that promises forever without him saying a word. It's a perfect slice of serenity... I wish I could bottle it and keep it forever. I can't remember *ever* being this happy.

* * * * *